ORIGINS OF THE MEDIEVAL WORLD

ORIGINS OF THE MEDIEVAL WORLD

William Carroll Bark

STANFORD UNIVERSITY PRESS

STANFORD, CALIFORNIA

STANFORD UNIVERSITY PRESS
STANFORD, CALIFORNIA

© 1958 by the Board of Trustees of the
Leland Stanford Junior University

Printed in the United States of America

Original edition 1958
Reprinted 1966

M. L. W. LAISTNER
MAGISTRO ET AMICO

Preface

The definite article was omitted by design before *Origins* in the title of this book, for it aims not at presenting a narrative account but at offering a critical interpretation. Specifically, it considers how and in what circumstances the ancient world came to an end in Western Europe and the medieval began. Of complete factual accounts presented in chronological order there have been a great many, some of them very useful indeed, but perhaps the time has come to clear away, as well as possible, the debris of views and opinions no longer tenable. A number of such views, some older, some quite recent, are examined in the pages that follow. In the course of this examination, every effort is made to clarify the general trends and bring out the overriding formative importance of the period under consideration—in short, to provide the setting without which the mere story of what happened can only seem puzzling and incomplete.

Despite all the efforts of medievalists to undo in recent decades the mischief wrought by writers wearing glasses of various colors, it has been extremely difficult to persuade the modern world to look at the medieval scene without preconceived notions. This is an old story in the study of history, and as sad as it is old. In this instance, it means that the West has remained largely unaware of a crucial part of its own tradition, a portion of its experience that may hold the power to render its own character more clearly intelligible to it.

Can the study of history legitimately claim to do any such thing? If so, it is very much to the point for our age to know it, particularly at a time when prophets posing as historians fill our ears with warnings of disaster. The most recent word is that the Caesars are coming back, are in fact breathing down our necks at this very moment. Can history make the present intelligible to the present? The best historians think it can. No one has made this point more plainly and succinctly than R. G. Collingwood. Asked what history is "for," Collingwood replied that history is for human self-knowledge. Further: "The only clue to what man can do is what man has done," and "The value of history . . . is that it teaches us what man has done and thus what man is."

It would doubtless be wise not to apply Collingwood's formula too rigidly but, mindful of Solon's warning to Croesus, to allow some leeway for the sake of prudence and human frailty. All the clues are not in until a man dies, and the same may be said of a civilization. The historian must get all the available facts, as much of the record as possible, and hope that it will serve. History may not tell us all we wish to know, but it remains our best source of information about man's potentialities. If we cannot obtain this information from history, we cannot obtain it at all—not by measuring the weight of ten thousand human brains, or by recording ten thousand outward aspects of human behavior, or by tables or charts or differential equations. We must go into man's mind, into the thoughts that have led him, and lead him, to make inventions, enter politics, waste money, fabricate superstitions, write poems, undertake business ventures, fight wars, and do all the other splendid, foolish, constructive, and criminal things he does. To elaborate slightly on Collingwood: The only indication, and it is not a guarantee, of the direction in which man (or a country, or a civilization) is heading is given by the trail or wake he has left behind him—the record of what he has made himself do or let himself be made to do in many different circumstances. Whoever would understand the character of Western civilization, which now includes the Americas, Russia, and much of Asia along with Europe, would do well to examine the record of its origins, the obstacles it overcame, the decisions it made, the courses it began to follow in the difficult time of its beginnings. This record ought to provide reading at least as interesting and informative, if less flamboyant, than the death notices published by the cyclical inspectors of the entrails.

Lucien Febvre, in a tribute to Marc Bloch's views on historical writing, observed that Bloch knew better than anyone that time stops for no one and that books of history, to be useful, must be discussed, plundered, contradicted, and continuously corrected and revised. Truer words could not be written; as Febvre added, a man would have to be stupid to consider himself infallible. One of my hopes for this book is that it will meet the fate of being debated, contradicted, and set right.

One of those best qualified to perform the last-named task is the man to whom it is dedicated. Although this essay should not be taken as proof of it, M. L. W. Laistner taught me a very great deal, including the most valuable of all lessons: that students, if they are to mature mentally, must learn to think for and by themselves. Nothing could have been conveyed more definitely and more considerately than this truth was conveyed to me by my greatest teacher.

There are many debts of other kinds incurred in the process of research, writing, and preparation for publication. I wish to thank the officers of Stanford University, the Stanford University Library, and the Stanford University Press for their steady encouragement, counsel, and material assistance. Many friends and colleagues have generously responded to appeals for advice and criticism. In this respect, I am grateful above all to Professor Carl Fremont Brand of the Stanford Department of History, who read almost the entire manuscript and in his recommendations gave me the benefit of his long experience and keen critical sense. My wife, Eleanor Carlton Bark, by her comments on the manuscript and in many other ways, has been of the greatest help to me throughout.

WILLIAM CARROLL BARK

Frenchman's House
Stanford University
November 6, 1957

Contents

ORIGINS OF THE MEDIEVAL WORLD

ONE

Perspective on the Early Middle Ages

The fall of Rome raises questions about the very nature of civilization. To the late Professor Michael Rostovtzeff, it suggested a lesson and a warning: "Our civilization will not last unless it be a civilization not of one class, but of the masses." He posed two questions: "Is it possible to extend a higher civilization to the lower classes without debasing its standard and diluting its quality to the vanishing point? Is not every civilization bound to decay as soon as it begins to penetrate the masses?"[1] These questions are worth pondering for the citizens of a democracy in any age, not least our own.

Elmer Davis, in an address to the Phi Beta Kappa Society at Harvard in 1953, a talk "somewhat motivated by annoyance with the doctrines of Dr. Toynbee," quoted Rostovtzeff's last question with the terse comment: "We can only say that we shall in due course find out."[2] In addition to making some allusions to Toynbee's views, he has much to say about the fall of Rome with pointed reference to the present state of Western civilization. In so doing, Davis, though one of the most intelligent and best informed, is by no means the only contemporary observer to hark back to the Roman fate with a questioning eye upon the present. Statesmen as well as philosophers of history and analysts of the present have repeatedly discussed our predicament in terms of what befell civilizations of the past, and most of these analyses have gone back, soon or late, to the one case about which we have relatively substantial information, the decline and fall of the Roman Empire. In popular utterance in newspapers and magazines, on the radio and television, this concern has been expressed in references to an impending new Dark Age of barbarism, to the new aggression of the East against the West and a return to despotism and slavery.

Interest in questions of this sort, and in seeking their answer in certain grim reminders of the past, has never been more lively than it is today. Were Spengler and Toynbee right? Are we to expect the decline of a civilization grown old and weary? After all, Western European civilization, which now includes the whole Western hemisphere, is centuries older than the Greco-Roman at the time it expired. In the last fifty years wars of a singularly ruinous character have both underlined and increased the signs of social and moral imbalance. Worried men talk of a return to barbarism and call to mind the fate of Greek brilliance and Roman power.

⌈ The gloomy parallels between the present and the Late Empire are admittedly striking, and conclusions based on them have been advanced with force and brilliance.⌐There is another side to the decline and fall, how-ever, a side that has been largely neglected: namely the slow, difficult emer-gence and upward climb of the Christian medieval civilization, the first stage of the Western European civilization now beset by difficulties.⌋Al-though much may be learned from the end of the ancient civilization, as much or more may be learned from the beginning of the new; and if warn-ing may be taken from the former, we may take courage from the latter. It is easy to forget that the classical world, in spite of numerous striking resemblances, was in many vital respects alien to the present Western tradition, whereas the medieval world was socially and culturally the direct antecedent and progenitor of modern times. Rostovtzeff was no doubt right about the lesson and the warning of the fall of Rome, but it would be wise also to consider how our own civilization came to birth, what its goals were, the conditions in which it then lived, the obstacles it surmounted, and the qualities and character that gave it life and vigor. If we are to consult history about modern problems, we must be willing not only to ponder the mistakes of the past but to consider its positive accomplishments and the spirit which made them possible. It is with these accomplishments and this spirit that this book is concerned. ⌋

When did the classical civilization end and the Middle Ages begin?[3] Dates aplenty have been offered. The deposition of Romulus Augustulus in 476 has long been a favorite. More recently 395, when Theodosius I died and with him the last brief reunification of the Empire, has gained ad-herents. At the other extreme, certain English historians would bring the early Middle Ages down to the period just before the Norman Conquest. ⌐Where there can be such wide variety of opinion, one is tempted to assume that little depends upon precision of dating and to fall back on the cliché that all ages are ages of transition, without "beginning" or "end." ⌋

Neither the search for an exact date nor the refusal to deal with dates has much to recommend it. The beginning of the Middle Ages was indeed an age of transition, but an age of transition in the narrow and proper sense, an age characterized by unusually rapid and significant change and marking a decisive passage from one stage to another. It was an overlapping rather than a sharp cessation or a timeless flow. It was a matter not of one date or no dates, but of many dates.

It matters when the Middle Ages began because when they began is inseparably connected with why and how they began, and also with just what the new age was. It would be as futile to try to understand medieval civilization without considering these questions of when and why, of how and what, as it would be to try to explain contemporary American civilization without reference to the age of European colonization, the Revolution, and the start of the westward expansion. To understand a given civilization or stage of civilization, we must know the conditions of its birth and infancy, and as much about what went before—its prenatal conditions, so to speak—as we can find out. Nothing could illustrate this more tellingly than the historical change under examination in this essay. In the gradual submergence of the ancient and emergence of the medieval civilization there is a remarkable contrast and interplay between old and new institutions and values. It is here that we see the overlapping referred to above. Naturally such an intermixture makes it impossible to date the beginning of the Middle Ages with pinpoint precision. This is also why different historians, some considering political innovations chiefly, others allotting more weight to religious, economic, or other developments, have arrived at so many different dates.

Clearly there is plenty of room for debate about the relative significance of various developments. This has not always been so. Half a century ago, George Burton Adams, then "the dean of American medievalists," expressed the prevailing view when he observed that "the history of Europe from the beginning of the fifth century to the end of the ninth" had been so minutely investigated that on all important questions in this field "there is now a nearly or quite general consensus of opinion among scholars."[4]

Fortunately, however, the assumed consensus proved to be not so general after all, and various specialists—economic, legal, philological—continued to make valuable additions to learning, many of them seriously altering historians' understanding of the crucial period as a whole.

As might be expected, the most serious challenge came from the so-called social and economic historians, such men as Bloch, Dopsch, Mickwitz, Rostovtzeff, Pirenne. In a general sense, their work was primarily destructive: it rendered what was left of the old consensus untenable, but offered no new consensus to take its place, no inclusive view that could be espoused by religious and literary historians, say, as well as by their own disciples. If the various specialists were to become intelligible to one another, an appeal would have to be made to general history, with all the risks involved.

This book is such an appeal, an attempt to try to see the problem of the end of the ancient world and of medieval beginnings as a whole. Its aim is to make clearer the relationship of the founding period of the West both to antiquity and to the later stages of Western civilization. Its method is selective and analytical rather than comprehensive and narrative. Its basic assumption is that the greatest value of medieval history is not its contribution to our great collections of facts—often idle, unassorted, unrelated, *historia gratia historiae*—but its contribution to the understanding of the confused, various, refractory, almost magical world to which the path taken at the outset of the Middle Ages has led.

American historians are fond of recalling the sacrifices of the Founding Fathers, and the legacy of freedom and dignity they bequeathed to their successors. But there were Founding Fathers of our civilization as well as of our country, and it is proper to acknowledge that Washington and his colleagues inherited a rich capital to invest. Such modern concepts as the equality of women, the rights and dignity of labor, the desirability of learning, equal laws, and the rights and responsibilities of the individual in society are not the original creations of our own time; they come from an old and tough tradition. Our concern here is with the seedbed of that tradition, the period of history when these ideas first put down roots in very rocky soil.[5]

TWO

The Problem of Medieval Beginnings

The English language has a clearly observable preference for the use of the plural in many terms where the other European languages are content to state the idea in the singular. Thus, writers of English examine beginnings or origins, they describe hard times, they have aims and goals more often than an aim or a goal, and in regarding their historical past they see in the medieval period not just an age but ages, the Middle Ages between ancient and modern times (another plural). Perhaps this preference for the plural arises from caution, from some legalistic insistence upon allowing for all possible contingencies. Whatever its roots, the term Middle Ages is rightly plural. There were several stages in the medieval era of development, and they may be as clearly distinguished from each other as from the subsequent stages of modern times. The *early* Middle Ages simply mark the origins of several basic institutions, ideas, values, and ways of life of the new Western European civilization which followed upon the decline of Rome in the West, and here again plurals are called for. But of this aspect of the subject, the beginnings of a new civilization, more will be said later.

There is another sense in which there have been not just a Middle Age but Middle Ages in our past and that is in terms of philosophical attitudes toward the period. To the Renaissance, the Middle Ages meant a time of Gothic barbarism and crudity. To a Voltaire or a Bentham the medieval era was an "Age of Faith," by which they meant an age of superstition, the whole dreary length of it worth not a moment of their own bright day. Some of the romantics, rejecting this as well as other "rationalist" views, went too far in the opposite direction and tended to view the Middle Ages only through pleasantly tinted glasses. They too found what they looked for, the picturesque pageant, knights in shining armor on coal-black steeds, ladies of high station on milk-white palfreys, castles, tournaments, maidens in distress, jolly priests and monks, quaint peasants, and a cruel Saracen or two.

There have been other kinds of Middle Ages, less interesting than these perhaps, but reflecting just as faithfully the prejudices, needs, and scholarship of the times that produced them. The "scientific" reaction has been of two main varieties, both somewhat emotional. First, there has been a feeling of revulsion against the ignorance and superstition allegedly fostered by an authoritarian Church, which were bad because they retarded the advancement of science, a term taken by natural scientists to mean primarily and almost exclusively knowledge of nature. It is a peculiarity of the holders of this view that they regard with great contempt the errors and blindnesses and blunders of men before roughly the time of Galileo, but are more tolerant of mistakes made nearer their own time. Second, there has been criticism along more or less medical lines, directed chiefly against the medieval lack of sanitation, general poor health, and susceptibility to disease. To the proponents of this view the Middle Ages were filthy by choice.

There have been other points of view concerning the Middle Ages, legal, constitutional, national, religious, but very likely the most constructive and historically useful has been the economic. Economic historians began to suspect more than half a century ago that important information might be mined in paying quantities in the Middle Ages, and they have ever since done much to show they were right. Among the most active of them was Henri Pirenne, one of the most distinguished of the large group of distinguished historians Belgium has produced in the twentieth century. Because of the brilliance of a thesis of his concerning the beginning of the Middle Ages and because of the enlivening and provocative influence of that thesis, more must now be said, in introducing the problem of the Middle Ages, about Henri Pirenne and his interpretation. It may be added at once that the Pirenne thesis, which twenty years ago was very widely accepted by medieval historians, is now accepted by virtually none without important qualification. This fact by no means destroys the value of Pirenne's work on the subject of medieval beginnings. He made a contribution of enormous value in challenging accepted explanations and bringing on a spate of critical examinations of historical clichés. In the tribe of the historians Pirenne belongs to the most blessed, for he raised questions.

It will be the purpose of the rest of this chapter to prepare the way for the presentation of the thesis of this study as a whole. This may best be done by a consideration of the nature of the Middle Ages and their relation to antiquity. This "problem of the Middle Ages" may in turn best be approached by means of a brief examination of Henri Pirenne's famous interpretation of medieval beginnings and its present status.

More than thirty-five years have passed since Pirenne first advanced the thesis which was finally presented in his posthumously published book, *Mahomet et Charlemagne*, namely, that the beginning of the Middle Ages is inseparably connected with the westward expansion of Islam and the destruction of the Mediterranean unity long preserved by Rome.[1] Mohammed and Charlemagne share the title for the reason that, in Pirenne's words, "it is strictly true that without Mohammed Charlemagne is inconceivable."[2] It was not the Germanic invasions that effected the great rupture between antiquity and the Middle Ages, not the Visigoths, certainly not the Ostrogoths, and not even the Merovingian Franks. It was the Saracens who made the difference. Their conquest of North Africa and Spain meant that after the eighth century the Franks held a dominant position in the West. The Moslems also aggravated the separation of East and West; since their clash with the Byzantine power in the East prevented the Eastern emperor from going to the aid of the papacy against the Lombards, the popes had perforce to turn to the only real power in Western Europe, that of the Frankish king, soon to become emperor.

It was thus, in Pirenne's view, that Mohammed prepared the way for Charlemagne and set in motion a whole train of momentous events. Government, the relationship of Church and State, the place of the Church in society, all changed.[3] Feudalism superseded the centralized State, and the ecclesiastical institution took over the leadership of a once secular society. The Mediterranean became a Moslem lake, and the center of Western European life was pushed back from the Mediterranean toward the North. A long evolutionary process culminated at length in A.D. 800 with the coronation of Charlemagne at Rome and the establishment of a new Empire.[4]

What has appeared to some students to denote a decisive alteration in the *status quo*, namely, the Germanic invasions of the fourth and fifth centuries, long before the birth of the Prophet, Pirenne considered only a superficial political novelty. Nothing was really changed by the Germans, who admired Roman institutions and wished to preserve what they had fallen heir to. They did not introduce a new form of government. Politically, they did no worse than to replace the old unified Roman state with a plurality of states.[5] In this analysis Pirenne seems to have proceeded on the assumption that if the Germans wrought no change, then no change took place. The proviso is fundamental; on it depends the validity of his thesis.[6] If further examination should reveal that even though the Germans themselves did not introduce basic changes, nevertheless such changes occurred, and had occurred *before* the Germans came in, the Mohammed-Charlemagne relationship would be seriously shaken. The westward movement of the Saracens and their domination of the Western Mediterranean would then be only part of a process which had begun long before Mohammed, Clovis, or even Alaric. It was after all Gothic, not Roman, rule that the Saracens displaced in Spain, and to the north it was not Gallo-Romans who opposed the new invaders but the cavalry forces of their Frankish masters. Gaul was continuing a change long in process; it was becoming France.

Somewhat similar doubts and questions are raised by Pirenne's contention that there was no fundamental change in the economic situation of the Roman West before the Saracens. The old commercial life continued, allegedly, suffering only a shrinkage due to the "barbarization" of customs. The same was true of agriculture, finance, taxation, and other aspects of economic organization.[7] Even as late as the seventh century Pirenne would have it that nothing announced the passing of the community of civilization established by the Roman Empire. "The new world" did not lose the Mediterranean character of "the ancient world."[8]

Others have seen the course of developments differently, however. Norman Baynes suggested some years ago that perhaps the Vandal pirate fleet had shattered the unity of the Mediterranean world in the fifth century, long before the rise of Islam.[9] François Ganshof and Robert S. Lopez have questioned Pirenne's assumption that commerce came to an end in the West after the Saracenic expansion.[10] Of the two assaults, one on Pirenne's treatment of the period before his crucial century, A.D. 650–750, and the other on his interpretation of the era just after it, namely, the Carolingian, the latter has so far been the more vigorously pressed. Trade did continue, and Lopez draws attention to important aspects of the problem wholly neglected by Pirenne. Thus one notes that fluctuations in the use of papyrus, Oriental luxury cloths, gold currency, and spices were due to internal changes not only in the West but also in the East, depending upon the efficiency of state control of monopolies by the Byzantines and Arabs and upon the system of alliances between the two Eastern governments. Lopez makes the further interesting point, suggested earlier in a much more general way by Rostovtzeff, that possible alterations in taste should also be taken into account; it may be that the Western barbarians did not care for the shimmering cloth and pungent spices of the Orient so much as their more refined predecessors and successors.[11]

⌐There may, in short, have been relevant changes in both West and East, which had nothing to do with the openness of the Mediterranean to travel and commerce.⌐ For example, Pirenne's belief that the irruption of Islam into the Western Mediterranean had an immediate repercussion in the Netherlands may be a distortion of considerable proportions.[12] That none but linen or woolen garments were worn in the West after the beginning of the Carolingian period and that it was Frisian cloth Charlemagne chose to offer the Caliph Harun al Rashid may quite conceivably mean that many of the active, fighting Franks of Charlemagne's time had come to have a high opinion of linen and woolen clothing, not only because it was cheaper or more easily available but also because it was in certain pertinent respects superior to Oriental luxury cloths. In sum, the curtailment of exports to the Franks was not simply a matter of obstruction by the Saracens of Spain. The refusal of the Byzantine and to a lesser extent of the Eastern Moslem rulers to permit their products to be sent West was also a factor, and perhaps a more important one⌐ Presumably the Franks had little that the Oriental world wanted and, as noted, there is at least the possibility that the Western demand for Oriental luxuries had decreased.[13] ⌐

Still another weak point, economically, in the Pirenne front is to be found in the short shrift given fundamental economic changes in Gaul in the period before the Franks ruled there, above all to the widespread destruction of the market for the natural products of the region.[14] It must be added in passing, that Pirenne again and again, just as in this instance, had difficulty with the paucity of available information.[15] An examination of the "evidence" he garnered from Gregory of Tours is likely to leave the reader with the feeling that not only was Pirenne able to make bricks without straw: he on occasion did not even require clay.[16]

⌐The two basic problems, the political and the economic, which Pirenne strove in vain to solve by stoutly maintaining that the old Roman system survived until the Carolingian era, rise up together, like a two-headed monster, in the form of the Merovingian kings.⌐For these sovereigns, in whom he actually discerned the image of Roman and Byzantine emperors, Pirenne made the most extravagant claims. They were absolute, being very powerful both in a military sense and, as the possessors of an immense amount of gold, in a financial sense. Moreover, the Merovingian rulers constantly added to their wealth in all possible ways, including the acceptance of enormous Byzantine subsidies; and like the Byzantine emperors, they made liberal use of their treasure for political purposes.[17] Yet the fact remains that these kinglets, so notable for their greed, do not appear to have been much interested in building up a livelier trade with the Eastern Mediterranean lands, possibly because it was easier and simpler to accept subsidies. It cannot be denied that they had taken over political authority and seized much treasure, but it does not follow that they had more than the simplest conception of the relationship between government and the economy of the state.[18] Their "absolutism" had only the most superficial resemblance to that of the trade-rich potentates of Byzantium. And to use treasure for simple purposes, such as personal advantage, to avoid an immediate danger, or to take revenge is not to understand and develop the sources of wealth.[19] To make of these petty princes more than pale ghosts of the greater Roman and Eastern emperors borders on the fantastic.

A further reason for rejecting the claims of wealth and absolutism made on behalf of these monarchs is that they lacked either the political wisdom or the power to retain the land tax. It is generally accepted that this constitutes the chief source of income in an agricultural society such as the Merovingian was as early as the sixth century.[20] Yet, in spite of their inheritance of a well-organized land tax system fully equipped with cadastral registers and a customs system for the collection of the tax, the Merovingians made little use of this major source of income and let it slip away.[21] This was, both economically and politically, a fatal blunder, for it led inevitably to the impoverishment of the monarchy and to the further fragmentation of the political unity of earlier times. The heirs of this process of decentralization were the Frankish aristocracy, and they no doubt understood taxation and commerce as little as their royal confrères.

Just as the Merovingians were too blind to see the importance of the land tax, to perform the public services which justified it, to supervise its collection and for justice and efficiency revise its apportionment from time to time, so they failed to comprehend the real nature of their sovereign power. This is clearly demonstrated in their grants of immunities, that is, the issuance of diplomas preventing royal officials from entering a designated territory and usually exempting that territory from the impost. These immunities no doubt helped to accomplish in reality what was never accomplished by official action, viz., the abolition of the land tax. Since other immunities exempted clerics and their agents from the collection of commercial tolls and other taxes, such as those on the right of passage by river or by land, the royal income was still further reduced.[22]

The question must naturally arise, why the kings so foolishly turned a blind eye to their own best interests. Pirenne's answer was, in effect, that the kings did nothing of the kind. The chief royal source of income, he insists, was the tax upon commerce, which, unlike the land tax, was very easy to collect and provoked little resistance. It followed that when commerce began to dry up because of the maritime expansion of the Saracens, the rich Merovingian rulers began to run out of money.[23] This in turn meant that their loss of economic and political power came about through no incapacity of their own but rather through the Saracens' action in closing the seaways to Frankish commerce. It was this deed, not royal ineptitude, which shut off the golden streams supposedly poured by the commercial tolls into the kingly coffers.

This answer evades the real issues. A key point, and one which Pirenne did not take up, though he mentions it in passing, is that the land tax was difficult to collect and occasioned much resistance. One must ask why this was so and what it meant for the kingship. It appears that the kings were becoming weak even before their commerce was afflicted with anemia, and Pirenne himself notes that the aristocrats, observing this increasing feebleness, took advantage of it to snatch more and more grants of immunity.[24] Why were the Merovingian princes becoming so weak that their own counts could prey upon them? An answer minimizing the importance of developments on the land, including the failures of the rulers to rule, and stressing the decline of commerce instead, could hardly prove adequate.

Pirenne further weakened his case by virtually dissociating affairs in the economic sphere from those in the political, although the two are inseparable in this series of developments. Again, though Fustel de Coulanges long ago called attention to the role of the Church in the granting of immunities and the weakening of royal power, Pirenne failed to give due consideration to the bearing of this fact upon the course of events. It is evident that the character of Frankish society was changing—witness the weakening of absolute, centralized power, the greater importance of local, landed proprietors, and the increasing influence of the Church in this social change—well before the appearance of the Saracens. Pirenne saw that the granting of immunities was a result of the king's weakness, but he did not realize that this weakness had been demonstrated early in the Merovingian era with the disappearance of public services. Nor does he appear to have given due credit to the testimony of Gregory of Tours, otherwise ransacked so exhaustively, that even in the sixth century the Church had stepped in to defend those whom the monarchy no longer attempted to serve, thereby early becoming an immensely powerful agent in the political and economic life of Merovingian France.[25]

To those who approach the Merovingian period by way of Roman history, one of the most disturbing aspects of Pirenne's explanation of medieval beginnings must be the scant consideration he gave to changing conditions within the Empire. This rather too brisk treatment may have led him to oversimplify and sometimes to take a distorted view of the later situation by passing too quickly over the earlier. The major question in the present context is whether Roman civilization underwent a serious and meaningful alteration between the second and fifth centuries of the Christian era. Pirenne seems hardly to have been aware even of the possibility, as he writes of the continuance of *Romania,* of a Roman type of absolute government, and of the Roman community of civilization.

Yet it must be allowed that one's understanding of medieval beginnings depends on how one looks at the early Middle Ages. Considered from the point of view of the later Middle Ages alone, they look one way; if the earlier period of Roman grandeur is also considered, they have a different appearance. Accordingly Rostovtzeff, well aware of the crucial nature of the changes going on in the Later Empire, warned against speaking carelessly of the "decay" of Roman civilization, for he saw what happened as a "slow and gradual change, a shifting of values in the consciousness of men." Nevertheless he held that "*ancient* civilization in its Greco-Roman form" disappeared, and he underlined "*ancient*." This disappearance coincided chronologically with the "political disintegration of the Roman Empire and with a great change in its economic and social life."[26] It was indeed "a great change" laden with the greatest and most extensive meaning for later ages. Virtually to ignore it would be a fatal flaw in any attempt to explain the problem as a whole. Merely to refer to the continuation of trade, largely by Syrians and Jews resident in Frankish Gaul, and to the continued existence of seaports and cities, could do little to account for a complex development. For so many-sided a situation Pirenne's "Saracenic" explanation was entirely too simple.[27]

Other questions arise in quick succession. The hastiest comparison of East and West, for example, must inevitably suggest certain lines of thought. Was not much more to be made of the contrast between East and West than Pirenne was willing to allow?[28] It is a matter of very great moment that the economic and social backgrounds of the Eastern and Western parts of the Roman Empire were so different. The way they responded to the rigid stabilization effected by the fourth century emperors alone serves to underline the point. The East had a long history of Hellenistic monopoly and control behind it, and it enjoyed conditions of relative prosperity. The East was more urban, the West more rural, and commerce and industry were much more strongly based in the one than in the other.[29]

One might also ask why, if Merovingian Gaul prospered as hugely before the Moslem invasion as Pirenne maintains, the Franks did not develop other steady outlets, through Italy and the Adriatic or by the eastward land route to Russia.[30] There was, in fact, trade along these routes, just as there was still sea trade from southern France. This trade decreased, however, well before the Moslem incursions, the reason being the West's low capacity to produce in the conditions that prevailed after the third century.[31] Gaul had suffered civil war, the destruction of its markets, invasion, and the feeble and careless government of the Merovingians. It was not Moslem closure of the seaways, then, or Moslem hostility toward the West, except at first, that cut down the trade.[32] Rather it was internal weakness and inefficiency, and worsening poverty with respect to export goods. The Moslems actually contributed, later on, to the restoration of commerce between the West and both the Moslem and the Byzantine East.[33]

The Saracens' quick commercial prosperity brings up another question or two. Pirenne made much of Mediterranean unity; it was supposedly a vital matter. Yet the Saracens, controlling only certain parts of the sea, were able to carry on a flourishing sea trade. It was not the unity of the sea that mattered so much, one must conclude; it was rather the economic status of the men who wished to use it. The sea was only a roadway, not a guarantee of commercial success. If the Western European peoples had nothing to carry across it, it made little difference whether the Western end of the roadway was blocked by Vandals or by Moslems, or not blocked at all, as in the fourth and fifth centuries and parts of the sixth. It should not be forgotten that in the sixth century the rich Byzantine Empire was able at enormous expense to invade the Mediterranean. Afterward, however, the Byzantines were unable to keep the Lombards out of Italy, and the Arabs quickly and easily wrested their African and Spanish holdings from them.[34] Clearly the Saracens brought with them an element long lacking in the too predatory economy of imperial Rome.[35] Saracenic economic enterprise, sustained by new-found supplies of gold, was to do much to awaken the West to a new and different commercial life.[36]

One of the most interesting and far-fetched implications of Pirenne's arrangement of the political and economic history of the Frankish period arises out of his assumption that there was a sharp distinction between Merovingian and Carolingian rulers in terms of riches and power. The argument would run thus: The basic change in the relations of king and aristocracy coincided with the Saracenic expansion, when the ruler gave benefices to his vassals in return for military service. Charles Martel introduced the practice with estates confiscated from the Church, and it was continued after his time.[37] The change, when it came about, occurred because the kings of the incoming Carolingian line, unlike the Merovingians, were poor. They were poor because of the falling off of commercial revenues that followed the Saracenic expansion and the closing of the Mediterranean.

To make the Saracens indirectly responsible for the inception of medieval feudalism in this way is of course misleading. The explanation completely disregards the inefficiency of Merovingian government. It is not enough simply to say that the Merovingian state continued the imperial forms of government, with the implication that the Roman system of internal administration survived virtually unchanged.[38] Far-reaching changes had taken place; there was economic decline, as noted above; there was also much less internal tranquillity than before; and there were undoubtedly important Germanic additions to the governmental structure long before the beginning of the Carolingian era. As for the alleged Germanic adoption and continuation, virtually untouched, of Roman forms of government, it is impossible to believe that the Merovingians could take over and operate successfully an administrative system which had been incapable immediately beforehand of saving its Roman masters from failure. One must infer that changing conditions had made the tool unusable before it broke in the hands of its inventors; it seems scarcely conceivable that the Merovingians could have been more Roman than the Romans. One must grant that there were bright spots of good, or at least strong, government under a Theodoric or even a Clovis. But what of their successors? Even Theodoric, according to Boethius, could not always control rapacity and corruption.[39] In local affairs Roman law and custom certainly retained some influence, but more as a brake than as a steering wheel.

Yet another aspect of the case touches upon the much-touted "unity of the Mediterranean." According to the Pirenne argument, Byzantium prevented the Saracens, after they had made the Western Mediterranean a Moslem lake, from taking over the whole area. Thus the old Roman sea became the frontier between Islam and Christianity and the Occident was separated from the Orient. In this way Islam broke the unity which the Germanic invaders had left intact. This rupture, "the most essential action" to take place in European history since the Punic Wars, in Pirenne's eyes marked the end of the ancient tradition and the beginning of the Middle Ages at the precise moment when Europe was being Byzantinized.[40]

It has already been suggested, chiefly through the illuminating remarks of Robert Lopez on Western trade or lack of trade with the East, that this "Byzantinization" was not a foregone conclusion. Moreover, Pirenne himself observed that somewhat later the commercial interests of Naples, Gaeta, and Amalfi led those towns to abandon Byzantium and enter into negotiations with the Moslems, a defection which permitted the Saracens finally to take Sicily.[41] This action reveals on the one hand that the Saracens were not wholly intractable, on the other that a conflict of interests between Western and Byzantine traders was not impossible. In the Pirenne construction, however, things appear quite otherwise. Charlemagne is portrayed as incapable of making the Franks a maritime power, despite the great profit to be derived thereby; Venice is shown to be entering the Byzantine orbit; and the Saracens lurk always as the dire danger.[42]

In this piece of detective work Pirenne did not charge the real culprit. Western Europe had access to a good avenue of commerce, and this access was denied it not by the Moslems but by the Byzantines.[43] It is true that the Moslems held the Western part of the sea, but after their initial hostility to the West and Western trade, they clearly had no aversion to dealing with the Franks and Italians. The reality was that Byzantium opposed the intrusion of the Carolingian Franks, who in turn were scarcely more energetic than the Merovingians had been in improving trading conditions. As for the Venetians, they would trade with anyone, provided there was sufficient profit to be made. They gladly sold Christian slaves and eunuchs to the Moslems, and they formed alliances as expediency dictated.[44] It should be added that in this eagerness to trade, the Venetians were not essentially different from their Italian, Moslem, and Byzantine counterparts. And the Moslems were no more free of internal dissension than the Eastern and Western Christians.[45]

It becomes ever clearer that Europe's political and economic center of gravity began to shift northward well before the Saracens took Spain, and one may even dare to suggest that strong spiritual forces also began to move in that direction at a very early date. This shifting of power may be detected, or at least suspected, from a careful reading of the *Mahomet et Charlemagne*, even though Pirenne, enchanted by his Saracenic theory, did not so interpret the evidence he marshaled. His views on early medieval, that is, Anglo-Saxon, Britain provide an excellent illustration of this preoccupation.

Britain, after its Germanic invasions, differed decidedly from the rest of Europe, according to Pirenne, for there a new type of civilization, Nordic or Germanic in character, began to come into existence. The Roman State vanished completely and with it its legislative ideal, its civil population, and its Christian religion. It was replaced by "a society which preserved among its members the blood tie, the family-centered community with all its consequences in law, morality, and economy, a paganism related to that of the heroic lays." Thus a new age was beginning in Britain, Northern rather than Southern in outlook and having nothing to do with *Romania*. On this view the Anglo-Saxon invaders of Roman Britain remained quite untouched by Roman civilization, and the historian had to conclude that "the Germanic, Nordic, barbarian soul, the soul of peoples whose state of advancement was, so to speak, Homeric, has been in this land the essential historical factor."[46]

This description is poetic, even romantic, but regrettably it is not historical. Though Pirenne caught a glimpse of the North-centered society to come, it was fleeting and he drew no important conclusions from the changing state of affairs. He continued to rely on his old assumption that the Merovingian Frankish society was vastly superior, because it was Roman, to that of Britain after the Anglo-Saxon invasions. The cruelty and viciousness of the Merovingian brood of princes counted for nothing. One must also wonder, though in vain, if Pirenne found the Anglo-Saxon soul more "Germanic, Nordic, and barbarian" than, say, the Lombard soul. As for the "Northern" character of the new civilization of Britain, here again one must insist on a comparison with other invaded areas of the Western half of the Empire and remember that, in some respects at least, the northerly movement was begun by the Franks as early as, or before, the sixth century.[47] Nor may it be forgotten, with reference to that strong Anglo-Saxon paganism, that the movement to bring the northerners into the Church was initiated by Pope Gregory the Great also in the sixth century.[48]

⌈Another oversimplification involves the Celts of the North, who are whisked out of sight somewhat too briskly.⌋ Unfortunately for the fixed interpretation, there were Celts in Britain as well as in the isles and on the Continent, and though not Nordic, they made history in this crucial period. By way of example, Pelagius, a Celtic monk probably of British origin, stirred St. Augustine of Hippo to the formulation of some of his strongest and most influential dogmatic views. It is equally indefensible to overlook the activities of other Celtic monks, notably Columba and Columban, in the sixth century, or to minimize the continuation of their work by Anglo-Saxon scholars, teachers, and missionaries in the seventh and eighth centuries, culminating in the outstanding labors of Bede, Boniface, and Alcuin. The isolated, "pagan," Homeric North could and did have an effect upon Frankland and even upon Mediterranean Italy before, during, and after the Saracenic expansion.

⌈Here, as in several other cases, the most surprising point about Pirenne's argument is that he was aware of the close connection between Rome and the British isles after the time of Gregory the Great. In spite of this awareness, he could conclude that "by the most curious reversal" the North replaced the South as the literary as well as the political center of Europe, and that this event provided the "most striking confirmation of the break caused by Islam."[49]⌋ The inescapable realities are that in Britain and Ireland the new civilization in process of growth owed much to the combination of Anglo-Saxon and Celtic vigor and enthusiasm with Italian and Oriental skill and experience in organization and administration.⌈It is reasonable to assume that the new civilization being molded by Celt and Saxon, by Frank, Syrian, and Roman, would have proceeded along much the same course if there had been no Saracenic expansion at all.⌋

This contention may serve to introduce a further test of the validity of the Pirenne thesis. If Pirenne was correct, the culture and the cultural directions of Western Europe as a whole ought to be measurably different after the Saracenic expansion, and the difference ought to be clearly attributable to forces set in motion by the Saracenic eruption. Pirenne consistently took up the problem of cultural change, as he did that of social change, by absolving the Germanic barbarians of responsibility. Thus he maintained that "the Germanic invasions could not and did not in any respect alter" the ancient tradition, i.e., the old unity of intellectual life.[50] In support of this view he could point to an occasional prominent layman, such as Cassiodorus or Boethius, declare that a simple Latin was written by Eugippius, Caesarius of Arles, and Gregory the Great only so that the people could understand, and argue that the Church absorbed the Empire, thus becoming a powerful agency of Romanization. He conceded that the intellectual life and the ancient culture were decadent after the third century, the "decadence of a decadence"; all he insisted on was that the Germans made no break with the classical tradition, that the break came later with the Saracens.[51]

Here the problem is much the same as it was in a smaller way in the case of Anglo-Saxon Britain. The essential question is whether the intellectual transition to the Middle Ages was far advanced even before the great Germanic inroads of the fourth and fifth centuries, not to mention the later era of the Saracenic expansion.

Unhappily Pirenne did not take up this basic question fairly and directly. Consequently the impression one receives from reading his chapter on intellectual life after the invasions in the *Mahomet et Charlemagne* is chiefly one of incompleteness. After referring to the general decay in science, art, and letters from the end of the third century, Pirenne proceeds with a brief sketch of intellectual conditions. Some, though not all, of the subjects that ought to be mentioned are mentioned; reference is made, for example, to the increasing Christian influence, to the growth of monasticism, to the continuing process of Orientalization, and to the deterioration of classical learning and literature. It is primarily the conclusions drawn from this survey that give the impression of distorted vision and unfinished work.[52]

A few examples will suffice to clarify the objection. In the Ostrogothic kingdom, according to Pirenne, "everything continued as under the

Empire" and "it is enough to recall the names of two of Theodoric's ministers: Cassiodorus and Boethius."[53] Two short, barren paragraphs are then given to these extraordinarily influential men, and even these brief references are so presented as to give a false impression in support of the thesis. For it is misleading to say nothing at all of Boethius' Christianity and his interest in the great theological controversies of his time, controversies which had a shattering impact upon the dogmatic unity of the Byzantine East and contributed also to the estrangement of the Eastern and Western churches.[54] No one would ever suspect from this little paragraph that Boethius has with reason been termed "the first of the scholastics" as well as "the last of the Romans." Cassiodorus is brushed aside just as brusquely. His devotion to the religious life at Vivarium and his patronage of monks are cited, but nothing is said of his extensive religious writings, or of his views on education, or indeed of the real temper of his mind. What is said is accurate, as in the case of Boethius, but since too much is omitted, here again the effect is misleading. Pirenne mentions, for example, that Cassiodorus wished his monks to bring together all the literary works of classical antiquity, a perfectly acceptable statement as far as it goes; but in referring to Ennodius, he gives the impression that ancient rhetoric was flourishing as strongly as ever, among Christians as well as pagans.[55] Obviously, it is implied, the classical tradition was still in full swing, with no essential change in mood or values. In reality, however, it was quite otherwise. Pirenne's construction ignores the moribund state of pagan rhetoric and literature in general and the bitter struggle, both long before and even after the time of Cassiodorus, against the profane tradition in literature, in which Jerome, Augustine, and Gregory the Great figured so largely.[56] To try to use Boethius and Cassiodorus as props for the view that society was still secular and essentially unchanged, to fail to bring out the very close contact of both men with the growth of Christian ideas and institutions in a crucial time, was a major error.

Similarly, Pirenne argued vigorously to show that the use of a simple Latin by such Church writers as Caesarius of Arles, Gregory I, and Eugippius did not denote any significant departure from the old tradition, but rather that the Church was deliberately debasing the language in an effort to make literature an instrument of culture, or rather of edification for the people.[57] This adaptation could then be described as nothing more than a continuation of the old Mediterranean culture. By this ingenious but unacceptable reconstruction Pirenne would actually have made the most powerful single institution engaged in the formation of a new Western society, the Christian Church, only an agent for the preservation of *Romania,* with all its classical and pagan tradition. The facts, however, demand a far different interpretation. The simplification of Latin was another indication of the cultural decline that had long been going on; Caesarius and the others wrote in simple language, because of the great increase in the illiteracy of the people they served.[58]

In this instance Pirenne again failed to strengthen his case, but merely described, without comprehending, the basic process of change which was taking place. Much the same is true of his other remarks concerning the use of Latin; for example, he interpreted the renewed use of classical Latin by clerics in the later Middle Ages as meaning that Latin had become a learned language written only for churchmen.[59] The knowledge and quality of spoken and written Latin, and indeed of vernacular languages, varied a great deal from place to place and time to time in the era from 300 to 1600 and later. The problem of linguistic change presents many complexities and difficulties, and it is perilous to generalize about it in support of a thesis. There is good reason to believe that written as well as spoken Latin evolved in phases from the classical on through late and medieval Latin.[60] Pirenne's view of the linguistic development was excessively narrow. What stamped men as more or less "medieval" and related to each other in values and outlook was not their command of language but what they expressed through it. In the time of the Hohenstaufen and Plantagenets, Latin poetry was written by and for laymen.[61] The songs of the Goliardi were also Latin, and scarcely meant for churchmen alone. Presumably the courtiers of London and Palermo, the wandering students, and the troubadours did not lose their "medieval" character because of the quality of their writing.

Pirenne extended his somewhat cavalier treatment of such figures as Boethius to the intellectual life of the period as a whole. He stressed certain kinds of evidence, notably the economic, to such an extent that he often largely, and sometimes wholly, missed the significance of important developments. Only a highly imaginative reader, for example, could suspect from reading Pirenne that the fifth and sixth centuries were part of the Patristic Age. True, the Fathers are alluded to in connection with Caesarius' simplifications, but the vast body of Patristic writings on many subjects, including dogma, is neglected. ⌐No expression of thought and feeling more clearly sets off the medieval from the classical than the theological controversies which raged in the fourth, fifth, and sixth centuries and continued to burn brightly long after. ⌐And later they were one of the chief fountainheads of medieval scholasticism. But of all this there is no suggestion in Pirenne's sketch.⌐ A reality of paramount importance in this crucial era was that only in Christian literature was vitality to be found; only Christians had convictions to defend or original views to expound.[62] Yet, just as Pirenne, in writing of the simplification of Latin, failed to see the connection between this development and concomitant changes, so he failed to assess properly the meaning of the new Christian literature or even of the growing institution of monasticism. No institution was to be more thoroughly part of the warp and woof of medieval life; no institutional change marks the break with classical society more sharply; yet Pirenne barely mentions St. Benedict of Nursia.[63]

Other improper omissions—improperly omitted because they bore upon the thesis Pirenne was submitting—might be mentioned in numbers. It must suffice to add that the great Pope Gregory I is banished with only a barren account, that St. Augustine of Hippo passes with no reference to his new conception of Christian history, and that other historians, such as Orosius and Salvian, are also ignored.⌐ The greatest puzzle of all, amidst so many omissions, exaggerations, and underemphases, is the description of Isidore of Seville, of whom it is said, first, that he retained none of the ancient spirit, and later, that he too was a Mediterranean.[64]⌐

The now familiar bias does equal injury in Pirenne's account of education from the fifth century to the seventh. No subject offers a better illustration of the far-reaching consequences of the collapse of the imperial unity so casually dismissed by Pirenne. Classical education, to the extent that it was a public charge, suffered the fate of other such branches of central and local government. After the early fifth century, therefore, the old system disappeared in Britain and Gaul, and classical education lingered on thereafter for a century in private hands, as in Sidonius Apollinaris' time.[65] In Italy and Africa the scholarly tradition lasted longer, but even in those regions there was considerable change, and classical instruction was largely dominated by men who were Christian leaders as well as learned men in the old sense.[66]

⌐The essence of the new Christian school, that is, the medieval, lay in the close association of literary instruction and religious education, in the fusion of worldly and spiritual teaching.[67] Pirenne would have it, however, that because the Germanic rulers employed administrative and judicial officials, there must have been lay schools for these officials.[68] The *schools,* however, as just noted, were religious, though some lay *instruction* remained.[69] As for the undeniably increasing Christian domination of education, this was not simply a matter of edification and adaptation, as Pirenne suggested in discussing Caesarius of Arles.[70] Rather it meant the construction of a whole new system of education for a new world with new values and aims. The evidence pointing toward this conclusion is abundant and is abundantly scattered through Pirenne's own pages.

In art, too, Pirenne could see no important change from the situation as it had long existed in the Mediterranean region. The process of Orientalization simply continued along the course set by the art of Byzantium, whose example in matters artistic was followed by the whole Mediterranean basin.[71] Here again, however, one must beware of an arrangement, no doubt unconscious, of evidence to suit a theory. Important changes did occur, such as the Orientalization Pirenne was inclined to brush aside so lightly, and others effected by the barbarians as well.

Classical art had been undergoing a change—not necessarily a decline—for some time before the Germanic invasions, certainly from the end of the second century of the Christian era, and the Oriental trend, involving style, spirit, and the actual artists, was also well established.[72] This change undoubtedly reflected changing conditions in other departments of Western life, such as the economic difficulties of the second century and the violence and disorder introduced by the civil wars and anarchy of the third century. Like classical literature, classical art was moribund at the time of the victory of Christianity; the zest and vigor had largely departed from both. The Eastern triumph in art was culturally a development quite separate from the classical Greco-Roman artistic achievement. The ascendancy of Oriental taste in art was not, therefore, merely the continuation of the old tradition; in reality it meant that an important change was in process in the Western part of the Empire before the invasions.

In considering the effect of the invasions themselves upon Western art, Pirenne again followed his established pattern. The Germans introduced nothing new but only advanced the influence of Oriental art, which in turn is dismissed as no change at all. The assumption that the artistic evidence also brought support to the Pirenne thesis was, however, highly question-able from the beginning, and recent research, which has been extensive and fruitful, has made it untenable. Quite naturally much that was Roman remained, for in most of Western Europe the invaders were a small minority, little inclined to mingle freely with the conquered. Gradually, however, an extensive modification took place, and along with the Oriental much that was new and barbaric was introduced. The barbarians had an art of their own; it was affected, to be sure, by certain Mediterranean and Oriental influences, but it drew still more, in a decadent form, from a great protohistoric art taken up by the Goths in Southern Russia.[73]

This much Pirenne would admit, but he would insist also that the art of the Germans was only a popular art and that in Gaul it was the work of native Gallo-Roman craftsmen.[74] These last points have been denied, however, by Henri Focillon, one of Pirenne's critics in artistic matters, and for good reason. Pirenne underestimated the importance of the social changes that occurred before the invasions and continued during and after them, changes that affected both the old population and the new, dominant minority. There was a pronounced movement toward the primitive, for which Focillon would make the Germans responsible. The old humanistic culture faded: the artistic absorption with the human face and form gave way before geometric formalism, and architecture yielded to the minor, decorative arts. In the Eastern Empire, which escaped barbaric domination but naturally not Pirenne's Orientalism, it was quite otherwise.[75]

In art, as elsewhere, the Pirenne explanation is regrettably inadequate. There appears, for instance, to have been in fact no break between Mero-vingian and Carolingian art, as there should have been if the "closing" of the Mediterranean was the decisive historical development it has been labeled. Moreover, after the closing of the great sea and at a time when Western Europe was supposed to have become isolated and thoroughly Germanic, the art of representing the human form reappeared in illustrated manuscripts and began to recover its lost grandeur.[76] The Mediterranean did not save Europe from "barbarism" in art in the period before the Moslem expansion, nor did its closing bring about the complete Germani-zation of the West. The conclusion must be that in art, as in economic and other areas, changes and new lines of development began before the Saracenic conquests and had little to do with the state of the Mediterranean. The term "Mediterranean," as applied to Western European civilization before and after the alleged closing, simply cannot be granted the value as a shibboleth accorded it by Pirenne.

Finally, Pirenne's method leads to difficulties in his account of Italo-Byzantine relations, chiefly in the age of Justinian. According to Pirenne, the separation of East and West and the alliance of pope and northern peoples were also products of the Moslem expansion.[77] There was unquestionably some connection, but here again an extremely complex series of developments and relationships is oversimplified and, in the process, distorted. As elsewhere, Pirenne tends to slight the theological history of a time when theology not only affected matters of economics, education, ecclesiastical organization, and even art, but often played a decisive role in the making of domestic and foreign policy. It has already been pointed out that Gregory the Great, rather than the popes of the eighth century, began the work of attaching the northern peoples to the Roman Church, and that the Lombards as well as the Moslems may have had something to do with separating East and West.[78] As for the secular character of the Germanic rulers before the Islamic expansion, a matter Pirenne made much of, it is true that the early Germanic kings, like the Byzantine emperors, interfered in ecclesiastical affairs. So, however, did later medieval rulers, and Philip the Fair was far from the earliest of them.

Too little has been made in Pirenne's pages of Justinian's careful negotiations with the papacy for the settlement of the Acacian Schism and his failure to placate the Monophysites.[79] Again, Justinian's later intervention and theological failure to win over the fiercely dissident elements of Syria and Egypt contributed to the rapid success of Islam in those regions; surely the theological background of Eastern hostility to Byzantium deserved some study.[80]

It is also highly doubtful that the "Byzantinization" of the West would have gone ahead on schedule, as anticipated by Pirenne, save for the rude interruption of the Saracens.[81] In this connection the historical meaning of Justinian's Reconquest is a matter of the first consequence. Pirenne granted that it cost the emperor dear in his struggles against the Persians and Slavs, but nevertheless judged it a policy corresponding to "the Mediterranean spirit of all European civilization from the fifth to the seventh century."[82] It would be more aptly described as shortsighted. Not only did it cost heavily in men and money, and also in the commercial sources of money, but it also contributed to Eastern resentment against Greco-Roman rule from Constantinople. Did the emperor act in response to Pirenne's "Mediterranean spirit" or to a fantastic dream of empire?[83] Whatever the answer, at that time the Slavs, Bulgars, Huns, Avars, and Persians profited most heavily from the ill-conceived venture. Justinian has been described as "a colossal Janus bestriding the way of passage between the ancient and medieval worlds," one face turned toward the past and the other toward the future.[84] This is an excellent description, though it is unfortunate for the emperor's reputation that he erred so often, both as a worshiper of the past in what he tried to preserve or restore and as an innovator in what he misprized and blighted.[85]

In West as well as East the Reconquest had consequences of vast moment, though not what Justinian envisioned or Pirenne believed them to be.[86] In Africa the decadent Vandal power was replaced by a Byzantine rule too feeble to stem the Saracenic advance. In Spain only a strip of coast was won, but the Visigoths were weakened enough to make them easy victims of the oncoming Moslems. The Franks were affected too, though indirectly; they were enabled to take over Provence from the Ostrogoths. In Italy the Byzantine armies finally succeeded in destroying the Ostrogothic kingdom, but at high cost; the peninsula was devastated, the population still further reduced, and the way prepared for the Lombard invasion. In short, the Reconquest backfired. Justinian succeeded in destroying the Ostrogoths and Vandals and weakening the Visigoths, but only to make the way easier for other and more dangerous enemies, the Arabs and Lombards and, to a degree, the Franks.

It must be granted also that the emperor seriously undermined his position by his concessions to the Persians, Slavs, and Mongols, by his vast expenditures, and by the antagonism he stirred among his Oriental subjects. The Reconquest, together with the emperor's religious policy, left both East and West much weaker than in the time of Anastasius I and Justin I. It might be suggested that if Charlemagne is inconceivable without Mohammed, Mohammed is inconceivable without Justinian. Such formulas are often more striking than useful, however, and it would be preferable merely to say that there was a great deal of history involved in making Mohammed, just as there was in making Charlemagne. In the period under observation the history of the West was closely connected with that of the East; and to be understood, the two have to be examined together.

That the Byzantinization of the West would have continued, had it not been for the Saracenic interruption, is unlikely. Not even Justinian could bring back to life what was dead. He could not conquer the Western half of the Roman Empire, for it no longer existed; he could not restore, by Byzantinization or any other means, a civilization that was gone. East and West were no longer what they had been, either in themselves or in their relationship to each other. With reference to this point, it is significant that a Latin-speaking emperor of Illyrian peasant origin, ruling in the East, could dispute possession of Italy with its barbarian masters. That his own armies were composed of "barbarians more savage than the Goths" makes the point indelibly clear.[87]

⌐Perhaps Pirenne's worst blind spot in examining the five centuries before Charlemagne was his inability to discern in that difficult time the beginnings of a new civilization.⌐ Gibbon's famous remark that he had described the "triumph of Barbarism and Religion" made a strong dramatic appeal, as the tough old age it has now reached clearly demonstrates. Pope's uncharitable line that "the monks finished what the Goths begun" makes the same point. The familiar terms "Spätantike," "Bas-Empire," and "Later Roman Empire" clearly imply that civilization was coming to an end and night was soon to fall. ⌐In essence, Pirenne followed the traditional path, adding only the new twist of his "Mediterranean unity" theory and his insistence upon an economic cause for the end of *Romania,* and with it the end of absolute, secular, financially independent government.⌐

It remained to account somehow for the far-reaching changes in Roman society, the persistent and successful invasions of the West by small bands of barbarians, and the tremendous upsurge in the Church's prestige and power after Constantine. Pirenne disposed of the Germans as noted above, by contending that they effected no change, with the implication that consequently no change occurred. He admitted decadence in the old Roman rule but maintained that it was still Roman and in the old secular way still dominated the Church. More will be said later about all three of these subjects, but particular attention must be called here to Pirenne's astonishing failure to recognize the immense historical significance of the Christian religion in the conditions prevailing in Western Europe in this period.⌐The history of Western Europe from about A.D. 300 to 600 can only be understood as a whole composed of two parts, each essential to the other: (a) Christianity, and (b) the more or less gradual breakdown of the

Roman local government and economy, the increasing self-sufficiency of an agrarian society, the oft-renewed disorder created by repeated invasions. The new society was not the product of invasion, experiment, and readjustment alone, nor was it the creation of Christianity alone; the two had to work together to produce it.

/ Pirenne failed to perceive plainly and to assess realistically the newly rising society for the same basic reason as Gibbon and most of his successors: he was blinded by the magic of the Roman name. Historical writing on the Later Roman Empire, even the most recent, is full of such terms as "a breathing space was granted," "a respite was gained," "the foundations of civilization were shored up," "the disaster [of invasion] was postponed." Only too rarely is it suggested that, possibly, what was crumbling away was beyond repair, indeed was not worth repairing and had never been all that these laments imply. Contrary to the traditional view that the collapse of Roman civilization in the West was a catastrophe, and that the fourth and later centuries were admirable primarily to the extent that they retained Roman influences, very nearly the opposite is true. The breakdown here simply betokened the collapse of machinery which could no longer perform even the modest functions imposed upon it. It was the end of an experiment that failed, and this failure left the way open for a new experiment with new creative forces.[88] True, certain bequests of classical antiquity served the new world well; they were valuable, however, not in themselves as survivals of a civilization that had ceased to civilize, but as useful adjuncts to a new culture. The best of the noble Greco-Roman accomplishment was not lost. "If it die, it bringeth forth much fruit" would not be an inappropriate epitaph for the doomed civilization.

It must be conceded that the circumstances in which the new civilization began its rise were far from imposing. Compared with the poverty and disorder of the post-invasion period, Roman or perhaps even Babylonian society might seem advanced. The comparison would be unfair to the oncoming civilization, however, if it did not go on to consider the possibilities latent in the new West. In a strange, indirect way the backward conditions of its origin proved useful to the Western Europe to come. [If it had not been divided, inefficiently governed, and poor, the influence of Christianity could not have been exerted freely and extensively. As will be brought out later, the early medieval society was a pioneer society living on a frontier, both geographical and intellectual, and engaged in advancing it. It is remarkable that historians of the West should so long have failed to apprehend this absolutely vital truth about the origins of their own tradition.

Perhaps the objection to Pirenne's slighting of the place of Christianity in this constructive process may be best expressed in this way: that there is more than one kind of economic causation, and that religious and economic vitality are not mutually exclusive. To say that the medieval Church occupied a leading position, in part because of the social backwardness of the time, is not to say that its influence was always and everywhere overwhelming and that there were no motives, interests, or activities except those inspired by religion; then, as in other times, men, even churchmen, were not always true to their principles, and the Church did not always win out in its struggles with secular forces. What is important, and what Pirenne failed to acknowledge, is that the Church was powerful enough to win most of its battles and to play a part in many events that were not, strictly speaking, its concern;[89] and above all, that in the fourth and fifth centuries, when the classical spirit was almost dead in the West, along with the Roman form of political administration and much of the rest of the old social system, the Christian spirit that was to create a new civilization was full of life and hope and confidence.[90]

THREE

What Happened to Roman Leadership in the West?

It has been said above that the early Middle Ages were a time of innovation and discovery, and that the regression of civilization in the West from the Roman level was a fortunate occurrence. The next two chapters will explain these assertions.

The evidence supporting them, much of it familiar in itself, though not in this context, is to be found in the social and cultural history of the declining Roman West and in the contrivances and products of the newly forming society, sometimes in combination with remnants of classical civilization and sometimes in wholly new and original forms. In this chapter the emphasis is upon the Roman collapse, upon what broke down, and why, and how. The following chapter offers a new conception of the dynamic character of the early medieval era, and therefore of the whole meaning of that era to later ages.

Political Changes

It is only too true to say that Rome paid heavily for the imperial adventures by which she forced the civilized world of the Mediterranean to pass under her yoke. In conquering the world the Romans lost their Republic, and in the fratricidal horrors, the political corruption, and the moral degradation of the century between Tiberius Gracchus and Octavian they lost their last grip upon the virtues which alone might have justified their conquests, both to themselves and to others. As it actually happened, their crimes nullified their sacrifices, so that eventually, with apologies to Horace, not only captive Greece but conquered Orientals and wide-eyed hireling barbarians captured their captors and came to share, or perhaps to rule, the Empire.[1] Order might be restored by Augustus, further conquests made by Trajan, and new cities founded by Hadrian, but by the end of Marcus Aurelius's reign the glitter of the Age of the Antonines so eloquently described by Gibbon came largely from fool's gold. Whether or not Rostovtzeff's thesis concerning the destructive rivalry between the city *bourgeoisie* and the peasantry and other unprivileged groups is accepted, the real catastrophe of the Roman Empire occurred in the civil strife of the third century, "which destroyed the foundations of the economic, social, and intellectual life of the ancient world."[2] Thereafter the Romans had, in effect, no choice, for though paths other than those leading to the destruction of enterprise, to widespread regimentation, and to Oriental despotism may have remained open, their leaders were unable to find them. Powerful administrators and reformers Diocletian and Constantine may have been, but their methods in an extremely complicated situation calling for extraordinary insight, finesse, and encouragement of individual talent were imperceptive, clumsy, and oppressive.

However we may judge the "brilliance" of these emperors and their successors in plotting a course, there can be no question that their work had extremely important consequences. They reformed the army, strengthened the currency, created a caste system, began the movement toward the East, and clamped a rigid system of regimentation upon the economic life of the Empire. Particularly important for the future was the fiscal innovation, attributed to Diocletian's reign, of the land tax based on the *caput* or *jugum*.[3] With respect to political, economic, and social legislation the central administration headed by Diocletian and his successors, in the West if not in the East, proved to be almost as helpless as that of their much later pseudo-imperial Carolingian successors. In the West the pretense of political unity and administrative centralization could be maintained only by ruthless violence and ironclad rigidity. Was the Roman Empire saved? If so, it was only saved, in Rostovtzeff's striking phrase, as "a vast prison for scores of millions of men."[4] It was not really saved at all, of course, in the West, but only preserved for a short space as if in a chemical solution, for the chaos and destruction of the third century could not be rescinded even by the most despotic legislation. Was Constantine's adoption of Christianity the act of an acute statesman or only that of a visionary?[5] Whether or not he acted upon the principle of joining an enemy whom he could not beat, that was in effect what he did. The political unity and centralization which were out of the question in the later, medieval centuries were already rapidly disappearing in the Western European parts of the Empire at the end of the third century, and the way was prepared for the medieval kingdoms and the slow process of adaptation called feudalism.

Yet the work of shoring up the imperial structure at the end of the third and the beginning of the fourth century should not be underestimated. Ferdinand Lot speculates on what might have happened had the Empire not been reunited late in the third century. Perhaps instead of the Romano-German kingdoms of the fifth and sixth centuries, there would have been several Western states much earlier, states with an exclusively Roman civilization.[6] Had this happened, some of the outward manifestations of the Middle Ages might have put in an appearance sooner—the political fragmentation, the general regression of society, the turbulence—but this speculation serves chiefly to bring out more clearly the significance of the reigns of Diocletian and Constantine, their absolutism, their reforms, their regimentation, and above all Constantine's conversion, which has been described, with no exaggeration, as "the most important fact in the history of the Mediterranean world between the creation of Roman hegemony and the establishment of Islam."[7]

There might have been separate Roman states; if they had survived, they might have retained much more of classical civilization for a much longer period than was possible in the West after the division of the Western Empire, but these states would not necessarily all have been Christian. The restoration effected by Diocletian, then, harsh though it was, and the adoption of Christianity by Constantine, mysterious though it may be, made all the difference in the world. They made it possible to replace Roman political with Christian religious unity and they gave the Christian Fathers a much better opportunity than they would otherwise have had to appropriate classical learning and turn it to Christian uses. These developments in turn exerted a profound influence upon the Germanic states as they came into existence. The fact that towers above all others is that unity was not wholly lost but changed, though in the most significant way, and that the change took place everywhere in a relatively short space of time. As Bury remarked, "The atmosphere of the age in which the Empire of Rome was dismembered was the christian religion."[8] Had this not been so, the Middle Ages, and therefore our own world, would be inconceivable.

Economic and Social Changes

It is obviously impossible to go far in this kind of analysis without bringing in the economic and social changes that accompanied the political and considering them all together. It is equally necessary to keep the state of the Eastern Empire always in mind, since nothing brings out more clearly the character of the alteration taking place in the society of the ancient classical world than the contrast between East and West.

The research and interpretation of the last half century have demonstrated the superiority of the East in population, wealth, political administration, and the solidity and stability of the social and economic structure as a whole. At the end of the third century Egypt supported one-seventh or more of the total population of the Empire; Syria and Western Asia Minor were also relatively thickly populated. The central portion of the North African coastline had a dense population for that time, and Carthage was one of the few large cities of the Roman West. What we should call large cities belonged almost exclusively to the East, Alexandria and Antioch being in the forefront with a quarter million or so inhabitants. Rome itself had perhaps close to half a million, but it was soon to yield up the advantages that held them. The depopulation of Italy and Greece, which had begun in the third century before Christ, continued during the Empire; parts of Gaul also were devastated and stripped of inhabitants. The destruction wrought by civil wars and invasions in the third century of our era seems to have been particularly severe in Gaul, doubtless because it was one of the richest and economically most productive, and therefore most vulnerable, parts of the West. In addition, this region suffered, like other parts of the Empire, from plagues, maladministration, and the paralyzing influence upon economic enterprise of the growth of the great estate system.[9] There was some recovery in Gaul, perhaps even an extensive recovery, but the aftereffects of the serious maladies of the third century remained, so that the state of the province was that of a patient who has improved but by no means regained his health.[10]

This basic difference does much to explain why the history of the West took a course so widely separated from the path followed for a thousand years by the Byzantine Empire. How did the difference come about? Why did the West go the way of self-sufficient, agrarian-based economy, desertion of towns, and decentralized administration, while the East remained in these respects much as it had been? It seems likely that the heart of the answer to this very important question is to be found precisely where the socioeconomic and the administrative meet and overlap.

One of the most perplexing problems to block the way to a clearer comprehension of developments in the fourth, fifth, and sixth centuries concerns the nature of the economy of the Later Roman Empire. Was it a gold economy, or a natural economy, or did it fluctuate between the two? Did gold continue in use in the Western Empire, or did it tend always to gravitate back toward the Eastern Empire and thence to the Middle and Far East?[11] It is hard to believe that in those centuries the Western economy would have retained a golden tinge so long, had it not been for the influence of Byzantine wealth. This relationship bears a general resemblance to that between the present-day economies of Western Europe and the United States; at least the resemblance is close enough for purposes of illustration.[12] In other words, the economy of the Western Empire, if not very carefully examined, may give the false impression of a robustness that it did not actually possess. That there was gold in the West in these and later centuries, e.g., gifts sent by Byzantine emperors to Merovingian kings, just as there are dollars in Western Europe today, cannot be denied. How much there was at any given time and how long it remained before finding its way back East or disappearing in some other way, is another matter. Such phenomena as the West's socioeconomic system, the strength of its *N. B.* towns, and the form of its administration are clearly better indexes of its vitality and productivity, and of its essential character, than the presence of gold.

It is only too clear that there is much about the economy of imperial Rome that we do not know and very likely never shall know. We do know, however, that for centuries the Empire's imports exceeded its exports, and that gold and silver were drained from Rome to be replaced by newly mined metal. When the mines could no longer replace the losses, the deficiency was made up by a depreciation of the coinage. The crisis thus produced brought on at least a partial return to a natural economy, which lasted in certain respects long after Constantine's restoration of sound coinage. Enough has already been said, however, about the heroic but only partly successful efforts of Constantine and his successors to bring about a real restoration of the economy. The population continued to decline, the expenses of the government did not abate, and poverty continued to increase. It was at this point that the government had recourse to the desperate measure of forcing men, for the preservation of production, services, and tax income, to remain in their economic stations, regardless of the individual hardships this entailed. Thus farmers were bound to the soil, urban workers to their labor, and officials in the towns to their responsibilities,

chiefly in the matter of collecting taxes. It is true that in certain parts of
the East small farmers had long been thus bound. The innovation lay in
extending the bondage throughout the Empire, including other callings,
and eventually making this regimentation hereditary.[13]

It is well known that Constantinople escaped capture time after time
partly by bribing would-be attackers with gold, whereas the West had to
get through such difficulties without that advantage. More than that, the
rulers of the East did not balk at sacrificing the West, even the city of Rome
itself, in order to remove a serious threat: witness the Visigoths and then
Theodoric; witness Attila and his Huns, who also went West after extort-
ing huge bribes from the Eastern court over a period of years in return for
sparing the Eastern capital. The meaning is clear: the East could afford
to buy protection with money; the poorer West could not, and therefore
suffered the fate the East escaped. We know further that in the reign of
Theodosius the Great, late in the fourth century, the gold budget of the
East was twice that of the West; that half a century later Marcian, after
stopping the payments of tribute to the Huns, was able in a reign of less
than seven years to save the huge sum of seven million *solidi*; and finally
that Anastasius I, at his death in 518, left a treasure more than three times
as large.[14] No such accumulations are heard of in the West. The West's
budget became even less in the early years of Valentinian III (425–55)
than it had been under Theodosius I, and smaller yet by the middle of the
century, as the regular sources of income dried up and military costs continued unbearably high. Meanwhile the taxes and demands for services
imposed upon the bulk of the population by the ruling class were steadily
increased with grim and ruinous inevitability.[15]

The East, then, was relatively well off, the West poor. In fact, the East
exerted so great an influence upon the economy of the West in the fourth,
fifth, and sixth centuries that the West has often been regarded as still a
part of the Empire. The economic vitality of the West was steadily ebbing
in this era, however, and from the West's own point of view the Middle
Ages had begun. The appearance of wealth and commercial activity there
is deceptive. The West, no longer self-sustaining and an active partner,
was in the process of being gleaned; its provinces were being plundered,
its cities destroyed or abandoned. As for commerce, even that of Gaul now
fell almost exclusively into the hands of Oriental merchants, chiefly Syrians
and Jews. These Eastern merchants, who had long thrived in the West,

undoubtedly continued to prosper well into the Frankish era; otherwise they would have sought their fortune elsewhere.[16] Their prosperity, however, is simply a testimony to the economic power of the Eastern Empire; they could not have flourished if the East had not remained strong and rich. They were a phenomenon produced by two neighboring societies, one of which has become poor but still offers opportunities for exploitation by the other. From the Eastern point of view they were bold and enterprising businessmen, capable of making money even under the unproductive, generally adverse conditions that prevailed in the West. From the Western outlook they were foreigners, resented because of their harsh business practices and arrogant clannishness, envied and hated because their ability, wealth, and Byzantine connections enabled them to take advantage of Western weakness and to prosper.[17]

⌈The evidence of commerce, then, provides no assurance that the West's economy was still vigorous⌋ Can this assurance be found in the continued existence of stocks of gold and silver? We know that there were still supplies of both metals in the West as well as in the East, apparently in large amounts, and that good coins were struck in both metals throughout the fourth century.[18]

We know also that at the same time the most alarming inflation took place. One reason for this curious state of affairs was that the amount of precious metals actually issued was not so large as the quality and types of coins might seem to indicate. Apparently, the emperors were not completely convinced of the need for a substantial and steadily flowing gold and silver currency. A further indication of this attitude is the government's practice of collecting certain taxes and fines in gold by weight; in other words, it would not accept at full value money which it had itself officially minted and issued. Moreover, such coins as were paid into the treasury in the form of taxes were converted into bullion.[19] ⌈The government's chief aim, therefore, seems to have been to keep gold in the form of ingots rather than to get it into circulation in the form of money.⌋ The explanation of this strange procedure may well be the fear that the metal would disappear into private hoards. Some of it did thus vanish, but some of it also was used as indicated, and doubtless some of it went into the black market and into secret transactions with foreigners.[20] It is certain that the situation was not healthy, and that the actions of both government and private citizens were ruled by doubt and fear.

Another evidence of the reigning monetary confusion in the fourth century was the attempt to achieve deflation by issuing large quantities of coins of copper and of copper dipped in a silver wash. The value of these coins, which formed the bulk of the money in actual circulation, was constantly changed, and of course the better pieces went into hiding. Attempts at reform went for nothing, thanks to continued disturbances and general uncertainty; the final result was inflation rather than deflation. The effects were especially disastrous in Egypt, where the drachma, which was valued at 4,000 to the *solidus* in 301, sank to 6 million to the *solidus* in 341 and 180 million to the *solidus* in 400. In this development, reminiscent of the German inflation of the 1920's, prices naturally rose to dizzying heights.[21]

This picture of the fourth-century imperial economy, with its plentiful gold and silver which was reluctantly minted and eagerly melted down when paid in as taxes, and with its strenuous attempts at reform and deflation ending in inflation, is already odd enough, but it is given a still more bizarre quality by the fact, already mentioned, that there existed alongside the money economy an extensive natural economy. Historically, the co-existence of these two forms is far from unheard-of; but it is nonetheless a curious phenomenon in a state possessed of considerable wealth and destined, at least in part (the East), to return to a money economy in less than a century.

It is now clear that in the fourth century there was nothing like a thorough replacement of the gold economy by a natural economy.[22] If natural economy is defined as complete self-sufficiency in which there is no possibility of free exchange, there was no natural economy at all in this period; there were only occasional lapses, at times when the value of gold sank and natural products were preferred as standards of value.[23] Whether it is called natural economy or only partial natural economy, however, is not important; what matters is that the economy of the Empire in the fourth century was in a perilous state.

The essential economic consideration for a complicated society, as the contemporary world knows, is not simply the existence of abundant gold supplies, but rather the ability to produce and distribute abundant wealth and to use enough of it peacefully and efficiently for the maintenance of an adequate standard of living. Obviously wealth or the portion of it available for those who produce it may sink considerably from time to time without serious damage to the society, provided the declines are not too drastic or too prolonged. If, by war or for some other reason, the amount of wealth available for the constructive needs of an advanced society is too long or too seriously cut down, economic chaos and political, social, and cultural disorder must eventually follow. This is what ultimately happened to the Empire.

In the vast extent of the Empire there were doubtless always some regions in which exchange was more often carried on by barter than by the use of money and others which were virtually self-sufficient.[24] What brought on the large-scale introduction of natural economy, however, was the crisis of the third century and the greatly increased power in the fourth century of the army and the bureaucracy. In the disturbed conditions of that time extremely desperate expedients were resorted to in many areas, as pretender fought against pretender and both struggled against foreign invaders. Some of these expedients remained, for various reasons, as an inescapable part of the inheritance of the reforming emperors of the fourth century, and the practice of the payment and acceptance of taxes in natural goods was one of them.[25] Thus, in spite of all Diocletian's and Constantine's reforms, the movement away from a money economy could not be stopped and the land tax was most often paid in kind. The practice of exacting requisitions in kind, so frequently relied on in the third century, was also retained.

Although tax collections in kind were elaborately provided for and carefully regulated, the system was very inefficient and extremely costly to both government and private citizens. In addition to the psychological disadvantages entailed by any sort of requisitioning—among the items requisitioned were beasts of burden, forced manual labor, and the staples of life, which varied in actual value from year to year—there were the enormous difficulties and losses (primarily from deterioration and theft) that are unavoidable in a system of tax collection involving transportation and storage. It has been estimated that under this system two-thirds of the revenue is lost in the collecting.[26] In addition to everything else, the principal taxpayers took on the burden of collecting from their tenants, the *coloni*, the goods which they in turn paid into the public storehouses. The State reserved, and sometimes exercised, its right to collect the land tax in money, but collection in kind was far the more usual process.[27]

Salaries were also often paid in kind. All the upper ranks of the civil administration had the right to collect their salaries in the form of requisitions, a right they were quick to abuse, and certain of the professions were similarly privileged. Even more important was the practice of giving the army its pay in kind; as a rule, soldiers received money only through unusual gifts (*donativa*). Presumably the army, like the civil servants, found it advantageous to be paid in natural products, easier to adjust its exactions to fit its increasing greed.

All in all, the practice was exceedingly costly to the government, and to society as a whole. The emperors were obliged to cut military expenditures by the only means left to them, namely by reducing the size of the armies and by enlisting less expensive barbarian troops, who were paid in land. This payment of the armies by requisitions and by gifts of land in the century that begins with Diocletian and ends with Theodosius the Great makes a startling contrast with Pirenne's description of Merovingian kings who paid their soldiers in gold. The reality was that in the fourth century the economic situation was already extremely grave. As Lot has pointed out, the system of payment in kind or in land has always led to the feudal or a similar régime.[28]

It should be reemphasized, however, that the financial retrogression of the fourth century did not proceed smoothly and without interruption. If it had, there would soon have been no Roman Empire left anywhere. For one thing, the Empire as a whole was not lacking in gold, and the financial problem was not insuperable. Indeed there was an improvement in finances at the end of the fourth century.[29] It must be very strongly emphasized, however, that this gold and this financial improvement were to be found for the most part in the East, not in the West. The West continued its decline, even though gold and silver currency was still issued there irregularly, and its movement toward natural economy. Only the East, although it still had its troubles, was able to set its house in some order, to collect taxes adequately, to curb the power of bureaucrats, generals, and great landowners, and to maintain and improve its armies, thus moving slowly toward power and stability.[30] It is against this background that the increasing barbarian harassments of the late fourth and of the fifth century must be viewed. The West lay there prostrate, a ready and inviting prey, incapable of defending itself; the East was weak, but the West was weaker.

The consequences of the experiment in natural economy were of primary importance not only in the economic sphere, but also in the social and political. We have seen that the introduction of natural economy at the end of the third century affected only State finance, not private finance, and that the expedient had its origin in the disturbed conditions of the third century, in debasements of the currency and in successive inflations. The reason the State bureaucracy labored to bring about payment in kind was that it suffered heavily from such disturbances, since its salaries never rose enough to cover the decline in the value of gold.[31] When salaries were paid in kind, however, the officials, and of course the army too, instead of being worse off than the rest of the population in bad times, were better off. In good years their subsistence was assured, and in bad years the natural products paid to them mounted in value.[32] Sometimes they must have profited very heavily indeed. Their profit, obviously, was the taxpayers' loss, above all the peasants'.[33] A struggle between officials and taxpayers ensued, centering about the question of how taxes and salaries were to be paid.[34] The laws of the Theodosian Code are, for laws, unusually eloquent on the score of the bitterness and frustration stirred up by this conflict. The depth of feeling that piled up behind the imperial rescripts comes to us only as a faint echo, but it must have contributed heavily to the psychology of desperation of the time, which in turn had much to do with what followed. As for the officials, the bureaucrats, are they to be censured? They were in a better position than the soldiers to gauge the effects of what they were doing, but they were desperate and demoralized. It is difficult even now to prescribe a course more conducive to the public interest and still within the capacities of human beings.

As for the taxpayers, fate was not kind to them in fourth-century Rome. Most of them, in the Later Empire, were organized in the colonate,[35] an institution with a long and uncertain history. In the simplest sense *coloni* were cultivators of the soil, farmers, but in the period under examination the term had come to mean much more than that. The *coloni* of this period were usually tenant farmers, but not a few of them were virtual slaves.[36]

How the changes in their status came about is impossible to say in any detail. In the Early Empire they were chiefly free tenants; in the Later Empire they were free men in name only, and in reality bound to the soil. It has been remarked that it is chiefly the juridical rather than the economic aspect of the development of the colonate that has been examined, for the reason that there is juridical evidence covering centuries, whereas economic evidence is very scanty, especially in the most difficult and interesting period.[37] What the legal changes meant, what economic realities prompted them is not clear. To say, for example, that a man, though ascribed to the soil, is free is a legal fiction.[38] The truth is that he is neither free to move nor free to change his occupation. In such circumstances, his nominal freedom could be little consolation to him. To understand what really has taken place one must know how he entered a condition of bondage—strictly speaking, of bondage to the soil.

It seems probable that the bondage of the colonate came about because it was to the interest of the great landowners. Obviously the *coloni* began to leave the land, primarily because the demands upon them for taxes in kind were more than they could bear. Their departure put the proprietors, who were responsible for collecting and paying the taxes, in an embarrassing position. Their only recourse was to pay the taxes out of their own private wealth and ultimately impoverish themselves. The solution was to forbid the *coloni* to leave their farms. Once that was done, the proprietor was safe, for he was assured of the labor and produce of the captive farmers; nothing thereafter prevented him from making up debts and deficiencies by increasing their dues.[39] Once this arrangement was put into effect, the tenant's position was irreparably damaged. He was completely helpless to act in his own interest, and those who had power—the proprietors, the bureaucracy, and the army—if they saw nothing else, at least saw clearly that a reversion to the former status would be to their disadvantage. This great social readjustment might have been justified, if there had been any power to call the State to account, by the need to assure continued agricultural production. We are concerned here only with its effects.

The hard conditions which reduced the *coloni* to servitude also affected the small farmers who were not tenants but owned their land. For them too it was difficult to pay taxes in kind; they too were damaged by fluctuations in values. The great landowner might pay his taxes in a bad year out of his accumulated wealth and hope to make up for the present loss by future gains. This the small owner, lacking reserves and requiring a minimum of income for subsistence, could not do. He paid the same large amount of his produce in bad years as in good, and since this amount was fixed rather than relative to his actual income, it is obvious that a poor harvest or two might well mean his finish. Hence the difficulties in tax collection.[40]

Since the State was incapable of helping the independent farmer out of difficulties for which it was responsible in the first place, he, like the *colonus*, had few courses open to him. He could join others in the same predicament who had become bandits, or he could seek the protection of more powerful men. In the long run it doubtless came to the same thing, i.e., to protection, for only in the most barren regions could landless men have long escaped the pressures of the State and of great proprietors in need of labor; and for family men even the escape into brigandage must have been almost out of the question. In any case, what happened is clear: more and more harassed farmers accepted the protection of feudalistic potentates capable of defying the State, and thus virtually sold themselves into bondage.

At about the same time, the *curiales,* the upper middle class of the towns, were made responsible for the collection of taxes. In time these provincial urban aristocrats came to form a caste, just as did the *coloni*, and their crushing duties became hereditary.[41]

The State's switch to a natural economy directly affected still another large element of the middle class, the officials concerned with the transportation and handling of taxes in kind. It was part of the general decline that decentralization went on apace, and that in its frantic search for means of keeping things going, the State had to seize upon every possible way of serving its immediate needs. Taxes in the form of goods were paid into government storehouses throughout the Empire. It was manifestly impossible, because of the state of communications and transportation, to send all these goods to the capital or even to a few centrally located depots, or for the government to know at any given time exactly what it had on hand. Inevitably, then, government wealth *in natura* was both collected and disbursed locally, and hence the central government could not retain control over its own financial operations.[42] It was obliged to work through local agents, who were paid by means of privileges and lighter taxes.

Such a system is clearly conducive to injustice and oppression, especially in time of war, when in some areas unusually heavy and unexpected demands might be made upon taxpayers and tax officials alike. It has been pointed out already that natural economy is favorable to a system of privilege.[43] Those who suffered most heavily and unfairly from unusual requisitions upon their services responded as the *coloni* and the free farmers had responded: they simply tried to evade their burdens. Since their services were as essential for the maintenance of the State as the agricultural labor of the *coloni* and small farmers, they too were subjected to compulsion and forced to remain in their corporations.

[Most of the foregoing is a familiar story as far as the specific developments go: civil wars and barbarian invasions, which put an immense strain upon the economic resources of the Empire; then financial experiments, depreciation, inflation, natural economy in State finances, decentralized control over tax receipts in kind; the reduction of the *coloni* to a state of bondage, the flight of small farmers to *potentiores* for protection, the burdening of the members of the urban middle class with heavy taxes and compulsory tax-collecting duties. Rostovtzeff's description of the Empire, after it had been reformed by its fourth-century rulers, as a "prison" seems apt indeed. Every man had his assigned place and his required duties; there was no escape.]

Yet there is something wrong with this account as it is usually presented. Not enough is made of the difference between East and West. In spite of all the warnings of such scholars as Baynes, Rostovtzeff, and Bratianu, who in their analyses looked to the Hellenistic and Roman past as well as to the Late Roman present, historians have continued to speak of the Roman Empire in the third, fourth, fifth, and sixth centuries as if nothing much had changed, and as if it were in roughly the same state of health throughout. Witness Pirenne's assumption that in the West the Germans merely moved into the vacated *palazzo*, whereas in the East the old rulers, save for dynastic changes, remained in residence. In both areas, according to this theory, the essential unity of *Romania* remained unbroken.

The conception of unaltered unity, along with all theories dependent upon it, rests ultimately upon the already mentioned assumption that the Roman Empire continued to exist for some centuries after the restoration effected by Diocletian and his successors. [I have tried to show that this assumption is unwarranted: that a major turning point in history was reached in the fourth century of the Christian era, and that this decisive point is best signalized historically by the reign of Constantine.] The differences between East and West have been touched on earlier in this chapter; we shall now examine them at greater length.

We have seen that the fourth-century emperors, in their policy of preserving the State at all costs, achieved success of a kind: their strenuous efforts won the State a respite, a chance to bolster its defenses to withstand the next onslaught of the dangers to which it had almost succumbed. It is pertinent, however, to ask what is meant by "the State" and "the Roman Empire." Precisely what was saved out of the wreckage of the third and the reforms of the fourth century? Certainly not the Roman Empire of Augustus, or of Trajan, or even of Marcus Aurelius. What was salvaged and given a new opportunity was the Eastern Empire, and despite the dreams of some of its later rulers, it is a mistake to consider it in anything but name a continuation of the Empire of classical times. The old Roman Empire gave up the ghost in the midst of the rigors and expedients and compulsions that bought new life for the East. In a word, part of the price of reinvigorating the East was the surrender of the West.

In order to see this, we need only examine the aftermath of the emperors' experiment with natural economy in State finance. To state it briefly, in the Eastern half of the Empire an economic recovery took place, but in the West it was quite otherwise. In the East the State had so successfully solved its financial problems at the end of the fourth century, to judge from the return of sound gold and silver coin and the increasing preference for payment in money rather than in kind (*adaeratio*), that the victory of money over natural economy was on the way to becoming complete. What prevented this from happening in the West, says Piganiol, was the continued presence of the barbarian invaders.[44] Significantly, however, gold and silver continued to appear only irregularly in the West along with inflation, whereas the Orient steadily maintained its gold coinage of high quality.[45] The great quantities of gold paid in tribute in the fifth century by Eastern emperors, the gold amassed by Anastasius I, and the gold spent and sometimes squandered by Justinian all speak to the same point, namely, that the disparity in wealth between Orient and Occident steadily grew.

The consequences of this poverty in the one region and this wealth in the other are many and important. Obviously Eastern rulers were able to curb tendencies which in the West had to be allowed to run free. At the same time, it is clear that the economic recovery of the East meant that it would again be to the interest of the army and civil service to insist upon a return to the use of money. Surely this is what the progress of *adaeratio* indicates.[46] As Sundwall has pointed out, there was no lack of private wealth and luxury in the West in the fifth century;[47] the difficulty was that this wealth was possessed only by a very few, as contrasted with the East, where the distribution was broad enough to leave some room for enterprise and initiative.

In the West there was no real return to a money economy, and no significant curtailment of the movement toward decentralization. The description of the Empire as a prison would apply to both halves; the great difference was that the harsh methods of the reformers worked in the East but failed in the West.

Why this was so we do not know. We know only that in the East the government's measures enabled it to restore and maintain order, to regain considerable financial prosperity, and consequently to relax the harshest and most dangerous of its restrictions, whereas in the West the same measures had almost the opposite effect, stifling and strangling production and putting power in the hands of the agents of political disintegration, the *potentiores.* This power the last Western emperors were unable to recapture, and their Germanic successors—with rare, peculiar, and short-lived exceptions such as Theodoric—fared no better. It has already been noted how little the Merovingians either comprehended or were able to correct the situation. Why were the late emperors and the Germanic rulers so impotent? It would seem that they were confronted with a situation wholly unresponsive to legislation or to administrative fiat, a condition specifically in which the economy had faltered, like a worn-out machine, and broken down beyond repair.

In the West the great estate tended to become self-sufficient, as governmental authority and the intricate and orderly commerce which required centralized supervision and the maintenance of stable conditions collapsed, and the kind of natural economy with which we are familiar in medieval Europe was well on its way. In Egypt, and presumably throughout most of the Orient, the situation was different, though there were doubtless exceptions in both halves of the Empire; for example, Italy in the sixth century was not self-sufficient. In Egypt, it has been found, a money economy survived and under Justinian rent was customarily paid in money. Even the strong Byzantine rulers could not put an end to bondage to the soil and to the privileged position of the great patrons, however, for the practices which made these ills possible in the first place had become too well established.[48]

Nevertheless there was a positive reassertion of imperial authority. Among other things, Anastasius I relieved the *curiales* of the collection of taxes, chiefly the *annona* or grain tax, apparently in an effort to protect small farmers and the municipal collectors. This reform did not always work effectively—there were certainly evasions and even backward steps by the government—but its general effect was to check the feudalistic tendencies of the great owners.

The Byzantine Empire continued to have serious economic difficulties, even under the efficient and thrifty Anastasius, and its finances were strained almost to the breaking point by the expedition Leo I sent against the Vandals.[49] Many of the attributes of feudalism appeared even in so prominent a region as Egypt. But these were only crises and trouble spots in a situation that was generally under control. The movement toward decentralization was only partially effected, as witness the continued commerce, the use of money, the existence of municipalities, and the efficient bureaucracy.[50] Despite such narrow escapes as that of Leo I, the Byzantine Empire was always able, though sometimes just barely able, to surmount its dangers and to survive as a centralized state.

Another illustration of the growing difference between East and West is provided by the municipal corporations, in which membership became hereditary and inescapable. This compulsory service, as noted above, bore far too heavily on some corporation members, particularly in time of war, with the most serious results for society as a whole. It is highly significant that the Byzantine government no longer had to require men to remain in corporate groups.[51] Mickwitz has pointed out the reason for this change: it was the Eastern Empire's return to a money economy. Thereafter the State could afford to pay in coin for necessary services, so that although corporations still existed and performed prescribed duties, membership in them was not compulsory. Indeed, and again significantly, members might be punished by exclusion from the corporations.[52]

The natural economy in State finances, introduced in the Empire as a whole as an experiment, remained an experiment in the East. The Western Empire was not so fortunate. It could not reverse or even check the movement toward decentralization, except in a few regions (notably Italy) which had close ties with the Byzantine Empire.[53] The small farmer was ruined; the middle class of the towns was harried out of existence. Both farmer and townsman could find but one protector, the great landowner, who alone had the power to resist the demands of the State.

It is an old story that the *potentiores* paid nothing like their fair share of taxes. The stronger the landowning senatorial aristocracy became, the less it paid.[54] Under fourth- and fifth-century conditions it could not have been difficult for the mighty to win privileges in the form of tax exemptions, either by intimidation or by bribery. Moreover, the government played into the hands of the *potentiores,* both by charging the urban *curiales* with the impossible task of collecting their taxes and by putting the farmers permanently under their control. It is no wonder that townsmen and farmers, hopeless and filled with hatred for the government they blamed for their plight, ran to the only person who appeared to have power, the local strong man. We learn from Boethius that even in Italy under Theodoric it was no different, except that now some of the great landowners were Ostrogoths.[55] As farmers and *bourgeois* flocked to the great patrons, their strength grew and the State lost still more ground.

In the West, in short, the experiment was disastrous. The State was unable to recover and reassert its authority; it grew poorer as the aristocrats grew richer.[56] The forces of decentralization won out. It is important to note that this economic struggle went on apart from the wars against incoming Germanic and Mongoloid tribes; though these invaders undoubtedly contributed to the breakdown of the government, it is by no means sure that but for them the State would have successfully reasserted itself in the West.[57] Had they played the dominant part in the collapse of the West, why had they not caused the East's collapse as well? The explanation would appear to be that the greater wealth and strength of the East were the really decisive forces.[58]

To sum up briefly, the collapse of the West as a centrally administered part of the Roman Empire took place before the great barbarian victories. The Eastern Empire was able to stage an economic recovery and fight off the invaders, whereas the economically impotent Western Empire succumbed. After the West failed to recover in the fourth century, the details of its fate were only matters of time and chance. The Western Empire ceased to exist when it proved incapable of resisting small bands of barbaric tribesmen.

Gold and Commerce

Before we examine the administrative differences between East and West, a word or two more must be said about gold and commerce in the late imperial–early medieval period. The matter is a complex one; the evidence affecting it is scanty and almost always puzzling. Two basic questions must be at least tentatively answered: How extensive was the circulation of gold, and how important was the metal, whatever the extent of its circulation? Here the primary need to achieve the greatest possible clarity in dealing with an obscure subject must serve as an excuse for some unavoidable repetition.

⌈According to Pirenne, there was an extensive circulation of gold in the Germanic kingdoms.⌋ The barbarians in Gaul and elsewhere simply took over the Roman system of coinage, based upon Constantine's gold *solidus*. The constant minting of gold which we learn about from the sources, the great wealth of the barbarian kings and the Church, the fortunes owned by private persons, the collection of taxes in gold, the vast sums distributed to the poor, confiscated, offered as bribes or given as dowries, indicate that there was a considerable stock of gold in the West (*Mahomet*, pp. 82, 89–96). Its source is naturally a very important matter to determine. It did not come from nonexistent mines; gold-bearing streams could not have supplied it; and even though some part of the West's "immense resources" in gold may have been acquired as booty, as tribute from other Germans and from Slavs, and as subsidies from Byzantium, this still does not account for its abundance. It will be clear even from this résumé how enormous Pirenne believed the supply of gold in the Western kingdoms to be. The terms he customarily used, "great circulation," "immense resources," "a really considerable stock of gold," present a glittering picture of a West, particularly France, almost rolling in gold, gold which must constantly have been streaming in from outside, inasmuch as the West admittedly had no large natural supplies of its own in ore, dust, or nuggets.

Whence came this golden torrent? ⌈Pirenne raises the question over and over, and answers it as often: from commerce.⌋ This theory clearly makes a mockery of the claims of Lot and others that the West in the Merovingian era lived under the régime of natural economy. Pirenne dismisses a reference by Gregory of Tours to payment of the impost in kind in the fourth century by saying that it applied to the imperial period (p. 96), as if this statement removed it from consideration. Elsewhere he remarks that the barbarians retained the imperial monetary system unchanged, and somewhat loosely cites Gunnar Mickwitz as authority for the view that the fourth century cannot be considered a century of natural economy (pp. 89, 98).[59] As observed above, Pirenne also believed that commerce both by sea and by land was extensive after the invasions, that this was a continuation of the late Roman imperial state of affairs, and that many traders, Jews, Syrians, Greeks, and Westerners, participated in the lively exchange of various commodities with the Eastern Empire.

It has been shown in Chapter II that Pirenne's belief in an extensive commerce was untenable; that the volume of trade with the East, which was small before the Saracenic conquest of the Western Mediterranean, continued in just about the same way afterward. Pirenne's basic error was his insistence that preinvasion commerce was extensive. If it is true that this earlier trading activity was modest, it follows that the Germanic kingdoms could not have brought in enormous quantities of gold by "continuing" it. There can be no question, of course, of their actually staging a vigorous commercial revival. Had their economic genius enabled them to soar so high, they would have given the Moslems a much harder time of it.

No criticisms of Pirenne's economic views have been more incisive and damaging than those of Norman Baynes. Baynes goes to the heart of the matter in saying: "The central issue at stake is the position of Merovingian Gaul, and in particular the question of the part played by the Syrian merchants of the West in the economic life of the Merovingian kingdom," for which Gregory of Tours is our principal authority.[60] As already indicated, Baynes sees nothing conclusive in Gregory's references to the Syrian merchants: no evidence, for example, that these traders maintained close ties with the East whence they had come, or that their numbers were being constantly replenished by new arrivals. Baynes shows further that Gregory of Tours knew little of southern Italy or the Byzantine East, and makes the reasonable assumption that the bishop would have been better informed had traders been regularly passing back and forth. From the occasional accounts Gregory does give of events in Rome or in the East, we may assume that his silence at other times was due not to lack of interest, but to lack of information.[61] Gregory is authority for the fact that some Eastern goods came to Merovingian Gaul, but he does not tell us that these goods came in large quantities or that they came directly from Levantine ports.

Gunnar Mickwitz strongly supports Baynes.[62] He points out, among other things, that there was but one sailing a year between Naples and Alexandria; that the ships engaged in this annual trip, though larger than those that passed, for example, between Rome and Marseilles, were not capable of carrying large cargoes; and trips made in short stages were more numerous and seem to have outweighed the long direct sailings in total tonnage. As for the Syrian merchants, Mickwitz suggests that the increase in their numbers in Gaul may simply mean that they left Italy and Rome, where their profits had declined, for Gaul, where they could do better. In any case, he finds no justification for speaking of Syrian merchants in vast numbers. The sources compel him to conclude that the volume of trade was small, and that the economic unity of the Mediterranean, as it had existed in the days when one great régime had exercised at once political and economic control over the region, had disappeared.

It is not hard to explain the belief of such sixth-century writers as Gregory the Great that commerce still united the former Roman world, and their casual use of the term "merchants." In some quarters the pretense of unity lasted throughout the whole medieval period, and medieval writers were notoriously uncritical and uninformed about population figures, the size of armies, losses in plagues, the volume of trade, and other matters requiring critical or comparative evaluation. It is much more likely that maritime commerce had been risky for some centuries before Saracen pirates took over the Western Mediterranean; and much more likely also that the Frankish West's ability to pay for Eastern commodities, either with goods of its own or with gold, was steadily decreasing.[63]

We must now look more closely into the gold supply of the West in the centuries before the Moslem domination of the Western Mediterranean. As noted earlier, next to no gold was mined or panned in the West; what gold there was had been either preserved from earlier times or acquired, by way of commerce, from other regions.[64] We know that gold was becoming relatively scarce in the Western Empire at least as early as the fourth century. One result was that the value of gold as compared with silver mounted; another was that the quality of gold coin was lowered. There is evidence that the quality of the gold *solidi* of Gaul was poor in the middle of the fifth century, and more than a century later Gregory the Great says these coins no longer circulated in Italy. There was a striking deterioration at the same time in the moneys of all the barbarian kingdoms. By the time of Charlemagne in such so-called gold coins as continued to be minted there was much more silver than gold. The same poverty of metal is reflected in the gold ornaments of the time. Obviously, as Marc Bloch concludes, the gold supply had long been dwindling when the Carolingians finally stopped minting gold coins.[65] How was this gold drained away from the West? Some, as religious custom dictated, was buried with chieftains; some, despite governmental orders, was paid out in tribute; some was hoarded, a sign of the general disorder of the times. Some was lost in raids or paid out in ransoms; some, perhaps, was used in trading with the northern barbarians. Part of this gold doubtless found its way back into the West, but there can be no doubt that much more left than returned.[66]

It is probable, moreover, that the West was importing more than it exported even before the Merovingian age, for which the excess of imports has been clearly established. Bloch remarks that foreign trade declined considerably before the Arabic invasions, and that these invasions, which Pirenne "rightly stressed," merely hastened the process. Thereafter only luxury items of small bulk and great value came in.[67]

It seems clear, however, that the reasons for the economic retrogression of the Roman Empire are to be sought not in gold and its changes in value but elsewhere.[68] The circulation of gold alone is a deceptive index; as Bloch has noted, even though gold coins of indigenous type were not struck in some parts of Europe from the ninth to the thirteenth century, gold in general and even gold coins, doubtless in relatively small quantities, did not cease to circulate.[69] We may conclude finally that for the West commerce did not depend on gold but gold on commerce; that in the period between 200 and 700 the West largely used up such stocks as had been held over from early imperial times, brought in by barbarians, or donated for some purpose by the Eastern Empire; and that the reason for this loss was the general economic decline of the West, including the decline of commercial activity. All the evidence suggests that the commercial decline was in process long before the Moslems appeared in Europe. It might be added that there is very little to support Pirenne's belief that the Moslems wished to cut off or did cut off Western trade; certain of the Merovingian rulers were much more reprehensible on this score.[70]

Natural Economy and the Patronage System

Are we to conclude that the West was reduced from the fourth century onward to a state of natural economy? The question is important, and understandably it proved harassing to Pirenne, who found himself obliged to answer it in the negative, at least for the Merovingian era.[71] The evidence, as we have seen, points both ways. We know that coins continued to circulate throughout the Middle Ages, and hence we cannot say that the money economy ceased to exist. On the other hand, we know that at some times in some places men either by preference or of necessity received goods rather than money for their services. It is useful at this point to recall Werner Sombart's observation that the significant distinction is not between natural and money economy but "between the economy which is self-sufficing and the economy which is not."

The basic change ushering in the Middle Ages in the West, socially and economically, occurred with the collapse of the old complex economy, an economy based on safe and relatively easy transportation and communication, characterized by open, plentiful, and rich markets, and permitting at least some specialization of labor and production. It is obvious that free exchange suffered very seriously when some men were bound to the soil, others to the performance of certain kinds of labor in towns, and still others to such duties as the collection of taxes. With the passage of time the towns themselves shrank and many disappeared; the future of Europe lay with men and women who lived on the land. For most people money simply no longer counted for much. They lived in more or less self-sufficient groups, and, like any pioneer community, they had to be more or less self-reliant. There was little specialization and consequently little exchange, and that chiefly by barter.

The crucial century was the fourth; the crucial step was the Roman State's switch to natural economy in its financial arrangements. Unfortunately, Mickwitz's epoch-making studies in this field have not always been given the attention they deserve, chiefly because two of his findings have been considered without due concern for a third, which follows them. The two are as follows: (1) that such scholars as Rostovtzeff and Meyer were wrong to describe the fourth century as marking a universal return to house economy, the truth being that the economic organization of the fourth century remained for the most part what it had been in the earlier imperial period;[72] (2) that there was an economic recovery in the East. On this point, he cites with approval the view of A. W. Persson and Ernst Stein that the transition to natural economy was only incidental, and that it was halted at the end of the fourth and the beginning of the fifth century by a return to money economy.[73]

To go only so far with Mickwitz's work, however, is to miss its full significance. He immediately makes the third point that there was a very important exception to the money economy prevailing in the fourth century, namely—as we have seen—in the finances of the State. It cannot be emphasized too strongly that Mickwitz attributed the development of the patronage system to the hardships arising from the natural tax system and the bureaucratic administration.[74] The *potentiores* gradually acquired small armies and a fixed labor supply; in the end they became strong enough to stand up to the State. The whole economic order was overhauled: on the one side stood the army and the bureaucracy, on the other the great landowners. It was perfectly clear to Mickwitz that even the partial and limited rise of natural economy in the fourth century was a matter of very great moment.[75]

As for his second point, that there was an economic recovery and a return to money economy in the East, here again it is necessary to weigh all his findings and not just part of them. He distinguished clearly between developments in East and West, pointing out that the Eastern emperors were able to collect great treasures, though only after the curtailment of the natural tax system. He never mentions the Western Empire in this connection, or any end to the natural economy in effect there.[76] Again, he specifically observes that in the West, where the senators represented the interests of the great landowners and often held the most important administrative positions, the government suffered dangerously from the growth of the patronage system as a rival force against army and bureaucracy.[77] When the great patrons became powerful enough, they refused to accept governmental burdens and worked only to advance their own interests.

Neither Mickwitz nor others offer any grounds for believing that an economic recovery in the East meant a universal recovery. Indeed, it seems clear that the emperors of the fourth century and their Byzantine successors, hedged in on all sides as they were by powerful enemies, some of whom were as well equipped with the knowledge and devices of civilization as they were themselves, did well to save as much as they did save.

It has been said that the great size and complexity of the Roman Empire were the basic causes of its failure in its ancient form,[78] but perhaps too much has been made of these factors. Too large for the state of communication and transportation in antiquity Rome may have been, but size in itself scarcely seems decisive, especially in a state which had been vast and yet had continued to exist for centuries. As for complexity, surely it is one of the inescapable conditions of an advanced society.

It would be wiser to examine the whole fabric of Rome's civilization for the fatal flaws which finally brought down the greatest single political organization created by man.[79] Corruption, greed, and inefficiency, much more than size and complexity, appear to be responsible for the failure to solve problems which should never have been allowed to come into existence. It seems clear that the cracks and fissures in the mold of Roman civilization first became dangerous in the economic façade, and that they were caused primarily by the Roman attitude toward economic matters: the penchant for exploitation rather than production, and its corollary, the contemptuous attitude toward labor.

Economically Rome ought not to have failed. The success of other peoples in areas impoverished and surrendered by the Romans suggests that the Empire's failure was caused not by its complexity but by its official fatuity and inefficiency. When maladroit Roman economic ideas and methods had allowed even the naturally rich portions of the Western Empire to fall into a state of such poverty that they could no longer pay for their defense, Roman civilization could no longer survive in the face of the hardy competition of the Germans. Lot was quite right in saying that the economic, if not the legal and political, bases of medieval feudalism were already established under the Later Empire, and that after the West had been broken into fragments, the *pars orientis* alone constituted *Romania*.[80] It is a matter of the first importance that when the Empire broke down permanently in the West, the process of barbarization had long been going on there. Naturally Marcus Aurelius's colonization of Italy and later importations of barbarians could not but change the nature of Western Roman society still more. The replenishment of depleted manpower must have had a good effect economically, at least for a while, but such effects cannot be limited to one aspect of life, as civilization after civilization has had to learn in the course of history.

The invitation to barbarian colonists let out a dangerous secret; it was not only the invited that took advantage of Roman hospitality. But even if the secret had not already been given away, it could not have been kept after the battle of Adrianople (378). It is the secret itself, its nature and its origins, that is important; the response to it was inevitable and, so to speak, incidental. In the eyes of Roman spectators, whose opinions are probably best known to us through the lamentations of St. Jerome and the dismay felt by St. Augustine on the capture of Rome in 410, the greatest calamity, understandably enough, was the barbarian invasions,[81] but their view should not be allowed to distort ours. Fortunately certain other literary sources, the panegyrists of the fourth century and Salvian in the fifth, reveal more of internal affairs, particularly the lot of the peasant.[82] The panegyrists tell us of the depopulation of the countryside, the devastation of towns, and the ruination of the populace, sometimes including the aristocracy.

The controversial *De gubernatione Dei* of Salvian, a priest of Marseilles, is in a class of its own. Composed toward the middle of the fifth century (ca. 440), it gives an exceedingly grim account of the plight of the peasantry. Despite the author's intention of reproving the Romans for their low morals and the deep feeling, not to say passion, with which he takes the part of the downtrodden poor against the rich and powerful, his description of conditions must be regarded as broadly accurate. Writing only some thirty years after St. Augustine began to compose the *De civitate Dei,* Salvian was no longer able to believe that the Western Empire might be saved.[83] So much difference could so short a time make in the way intelligent men interpreted the life of their times.

This view of an important part of Western society in the fifth century has extraordinary value for us, even after all allowances have been made for the human tendency in times of trouble to make things out a little worse than they actually are. For Salvian's fiery work corroborates the evidence of the law codes and financial decrees, putting flesh on what otherwise remains, at least to some extent, dry bones. Much of the time Salvian writes from his own knowledge, speaking not of abstractions but of what he saw happening to real human beings. The society he portrays is in a state of dissolution—and reconstruction. The legal processes begun in the late third and the fourth centuries, which were to lead to patronage and the enslavement of the *coloni,* were now exerting their full effects. The remnants of the *curiales* were still responsible for the collection of taxes in prescribed areas, and the great proprietors were thriving under the system designed to stabilize the labor supply and bring in the maximum amount of taxes. Only, as Salvian shows us, these laws and taxes, bad enough in themselves, were not applied with equity. Those least able to pay paid the most, and the wealthy found ways to shift the burden to the poor. Even when the government attempted to rectify this situation to a certain extent, the powerful contrived to cheat the peasantry and add to their own wealth (*De gubernatione Dei,* IV, 31). Because of the *curiales'* injustice and tyranny, our moralist bears them no love (III, 50; V, 18), but at the same time he is aware of the sad condition of the cities and their people (e.g., IV, 21; VI, 80; VI, 88–89). He denounces the *curiales* along with officials, soldiers, and businessmen. The last-named he accuses of fraud and perjury (III, 50), and he makes particular mention of the crowds of Syrian merchants, "which have taken over the major part of all our towns" and live by trickery and falsehood (IV, 69).

Altogether, however, *curiales* and merchants engage but a small portion of Salvian's attention. He describes the wretched state of the cities, given up to the rapine of soldiers and barbarians, burned, and pillaged, some of them repeatedly, as in the case of Trèves, and some of them completely destroyed (VI, 39, 67–69, 74–75, 77, 80, 82–84); but he is interested primarily in causes, in explaining why these abominations had taken place, and he finds the answer in the unending corruption of the Romans. It was to punish the Romans, indeed to destroy them, that the barbarians were sent to Gaul, to Spain, to all the West (VI, 67–69; VII, 50–54). It is significant that when Salvian turns from the wantonness and sexual depravity of the Romans, from their brutality and love of cruel shows, to the greed, deceit, and hardheartedness that ruled their social and economic lives, he gives much more attention to the fate of the landed population than to that of the town dwellers. He believed that the small farmers were the real producers (e.g., V, 35).

He seems to have grasped also, doubtless dimly enough, that the next acts of the historical drama were to be played on this rural stage, to judge from his remarks about the social crisis involved in the triumph of the patronage system. More than a century before, in 328, Constantine himself had conceded that some of the *potentiores* could be controlled only by the Pretorian Prefect and the Emperor.[84] How much more powerful must these princelings have become in the West by Salvian's time! Salvian is silent on this particular matter, but he reveals plainly, nevertheless, that Roman society had crumbled away internally, and he was convinced that there could be no restoration of things as they had been. This is doubtless why his sorrowful account of their destruction is reminiscent of Tiberius Gracchus's famous description of the ruined farmer-veterans of Italy at the beginning of the last century of the Roman Republic, as told by Plutarch.

How were Salvian's yeomen led to ruin? When he describes the Roman commonwealth as being strangled by taxes, he adds that the poor are "assassinated" by having to pay the taxes of the rich (IV, 30). Their wealthy assassins are the same men who cheat the poor when the government tries to help the ruined cities. The wretches are taxpayers only when the taxes are collected; when alleviations are being apportioned, the poor are ignored by the few who make the decisions for all (IV, 31; V, 33-35).

Salvian is perhaps too fond of saying that the *potentiores* assassinated the poor, but if even half of his observations are accurate, the expression is well chosen. For what were the poor to do in the circumstances? Some, we learn, fled from their old homes and lived as refugees among the barbarians—a distasteful step, according to Salvian, who refers pointedly to the barbarians' unfamiliar habits and even to their unpleasant odor, but better than submitting to the injustice that prevailed among the Romans (V, 21).[85] Others joined the Bagaudae or peasant-brigands. This also was a serious step; the Bagaudae lived no better than the barbarians and were scorned as rebels by the Romans who had hounded them out of society. At first they were few, but men who had not joined them before were joining them in Salvian's time; and still more would, he says, if they were able (V, 24-26).

The reason why the rest did not flee to the brigands or barbarians is simply explained: they could not take with them their miserable possessions, homes, and families. In an effort to save what they could, they took the only course left and put themselves under the protection of the powerful (V, 38). The price of this protection was realistically high. As Salvian describes the process, the small landowners were permitted to remain on their land under the protection of the great, but upon the death of the small owner the land became the patron's to do with as he liked; in effect, parents bought succor for themselves by condemning their children to a life of beggary (V, 39). Salvian leaves it to his readers to calculate the bitterness and despair of men who could not bear to desert their dependents and yet could scarcely bear to stay with them in their wretchedness.

A further illustration of the almost complete helplessness of the small owners is that after losing their holdings they still had to pay taxes on them (V, 42-43). This meant that the children of owners who had bought protection lost not only the family farm but soon whatever small movable possessions the family might have been able to preserve. Obviously when this state had been reached, ordinary men could no longer have any interest in the maintenance of the Roman jurisdiction that had ruined them. They would prefer to live under the rule of the barbarians, who treated former Romans better than the Romans treated their own people (V, 36–37). Some of the small owners, assessing the situation accurately, took the final step, went to the estates of the great lords, and became their *coloni* (V, 43).

Salvian makes the final point in this account with great feeling: that these wretched men were compelled to give up not only their homes and possessions, the patrimonies and the future welfare that should have gone to their children, but even their status as free men. They lost their rank and place in society and entered a servile state, separated as exiles not merely from their property but from their very selves (V, 44). Ultimately they found themselves received as outsiders, natives no longer but newcomers now, changed into beasts as if by Circe's magic, treated as property, turned into slaves (V, 45).

In spite of Salvian's religious point of view, in spite of his moral (that the Romans were coming to know for themselves the bitterness of exile and enslavement, which they had formerly dealt out so lavishly to others), the acuteness and perspicacity of the account make it deeply impressive as a historical document. Salvian was quite aware that the Romans, even when faced by a foreign enemy, instead of standing shoulder to shoulder, were betraying each other—unlike the barbarians, who respected the bonds of tribal membership and the rule of one king, and lived together in amity (V, 15).[86] Among the Romans, not merely fellow citizens but even neighbors, and, worst of all, relatives, turned on each other (V, 16). Again and again we are shown the deadening and demoralizing effect of this strife. Cities were left unguarded even when the barbarians were almost in sight, and "though doubtless no one wished to die, still no one did anything to avoid death" (VI, 80). Salvian was convinced that the great proprietors could not profit in the long run from the course they were following, at least as members of a civilized, "Roman" society: "I ask you what madness or blindness it is to believe that private fortunes can survive when the commonwealth has been reduced to want and beggary" (I, 11).

There can be no doubt that Salvian saw in the gradual disappearance of small, independent farmers and their absorption into the system of huge rural estates the clearest sign of the decadence of the Western Empire.[87]

Divided into two unequal groups, a small group of great proprietors and a large group of their tenants, society was already medieval. Things were to change considerably in the course of the next millennium, but by Salvian's time the pattern of rural life was formed for the great majority of Europeans. They lived on land which they did not own or control, performing services and paying taxes, usually in kind, according to established custom, with such variations as the lord of the estate decreed. Though in the course of centuries the life of these men was greatly affected by political events, the continuance or resurgence of Eastern Roman authority in this or that area, the development of feudalism, new barbarian invasions, and eventually in some regions the slow growth of royal power, it was for most of them the superficial aspects of life rather than the fundamentals that changed.

For a time towns in some numbers continued to exist in the West, and after the tenth century towns were built or rebuilt to meet new needs, but for a thousand years in most of the West and for much longer in some parts of it life was predominantly rural. Not all the West was being transformed by Salvian's time; parts of Italy, for example, never lost touch with the East, and there were local differences elsewhere. But the great social change which Salvian saw taking place with such horrifying speed, and which he described with such impressive clarity, had long been on the way.

It is impossible not to see in this social change of the fourth and fifth centuries a revolution in reverse, or to use a biological term, a social devolution. The history of recent centuries is so studded with revolutions of a different kind that their general pattern is quite familiar. Economic conditions improve; the standard of living of the masses is raised; then an opportunity is presented, sometimes deliberately by benevolent liberals, sometimes accidentally by discoveries, wars, plagues, inventions, for a social advance great enough to be called a revolution. Our age has accordingly become so accustomed to thinking of revolutions as progressive that we may not quickly recognize a retrogressive revolution. Yet this is precisely what was taking place in Western, and for a time in Eastern, society in the fourth and fifth centuries.[88]

Some General Observations on Late Roman Society

Other sources confirm Salvian's observations about the superior justice and decency of the barbarians. St. Augustine's friend Orosius, writing a generation earlier than Salvian, tells of Romans in his time who preferred freedom in poverty among the barbarians to life with their own people under the burden of taxation.[89] A generation after Salvian, with Roman maladministration as bad as ever, even Sidonius Apollinaris—a man far more conscious than Salvian of some of the disagreeable mannerisms and customs of the Germans—could describe the Visigoth Theodoric II as an admirable personage, modest, handsome, industrious, good-natured, temperate, and conscientious.[90] Cassiodorus in the sixth century was only one of many Romans of distinction to follow a deliberate policy of friendship and collaboration with the intruders. Many Romans, of course, including some of those who had kind words for the Germans' vigor, courage, and diligence, were proud of their Roman ancestry and looked down upon their guests as crude, loutish upstarts: we need mention only the anti-German group in Stilicho's time, the Roman aristocratic faction which hoped for a union with the Eastern Empire during the reign of Theodoric the Great, and the views expressed by Sidonius in his panegyrics on Avitus and Majorian. The stark reality, however, was that the Romans of the West had no choice but to live side by side with the barbarians, usually in a somewhat subservient position, and that they had been adjusting themselves to this state of affairs long before Salvian wrote of their frequent desertion to their former enemies.

We have no orderly account of the process of change and adjustment in the newly forming society of the West. For one thing, what writers there were had other interests: witness the notoriously uninformative Sidonius. More important, perhaps, the process itself was not orderly; it fluctuated constantly with the rise and decline of imperial military fortunes, the movement of barbarian peoples, and the changing alliances between the Empire and barbarian chieftains and between one barbarian people and another. All we can say with certainty is that under the surface, slowly but in the long run steadily, the old order was breaking up and being replaced, not all at once but piece by piece, by a new way of life. Few Romans, even among the better educated, understood that they were protagonists in one of the greatest revolutions ever to take place in the history of Western civilization. For the most part, ordinary Romans in the fifth century knew only that the Roman armies were more and more composed of Germans and led by Germans; that despite these armies, the barbarians continued to move into Roman territory and take over land for their own use; that in those regions of the West remaining under Roman jurisdiction corruption and injustice had long been the order of the day; and that the burden of taxation was insupportable.

"Romans" still existed, greatly outnumbering the Germans in their midst and on their frontiers; Roman buildings, Roman clothing, Roman officials, were everywhere in evidence; feudalism, considered either in the social and political or in the legal sense, still lay far in the future. Everywhere Rome, though embattled, seemingly lived on. But everywhere, behind the façade of continuing Roman phenomena, the old, classical, pagan Roman world of the West was dead. Nothing could have revived it, and nothing could have rendered it more lifeless, neither Germans, nor Huns, nor Slavs, nor Saracens. The Germans were present at the celebration of the obsequies; the Saracens appeared long after the burial had taken place.

There is little to be said for the idea that no really significant change need be recognized until it is fully accomplished. As a rule, historical change, even in periods properly called transitional, takes place slowly, and every social and cultural development of great moment has a long history behind it. Thus in the period of the declining classical and the rising medieval civilization of the West, the new society—call it feudal, or agrarian, or simple, or what you will—was taking shape long before anything like its final form was achieved. If we cannot call Western society medieval until the appearance of full-fledged feudalism, complete with immunities, oaths of fealty, and military benefices, we are left to face a vast and ill-explained hiatus after the expiration of the old civilization in the West. Moreover, this full-blown type of feudalism hardly appears before it begins in turn to change.

The political weaknesses, affecting both domestic and foreign affairs, which accompanied the social and economic retrogression require no further emphasis. Early in the fourth century came Constantine's conversion to Christianity. Half a century after his transfer of the capital to the East occurrred the disaster of Adrianople, followed only a generation later by Alaric's capture of the Eternal City. So portentously and so quickly appeared the signs of Roman weakness in the West and of the onrushing fate of the Western Empire! At first sight it scarcely seems remarkable, though actually it was very remarkable indeed, that even so trenchant a mind as St. Augustine's should have perceived something of the shape of things to come and should have created a whole new philosophy of history to explain it.

Much has been said in the past about the enormous influence of Roman civilization upon the Germans. Perhaps too little has been made of the fact that the Rome the intruders knew was in dissolution, ground down by failure and despair, losing heart, ready to grasp at any chance for survival. To be sure, some of the Romans among whom the invaders lived in Gaul, Spain, and Italy were men of substance, culture, and no little arrogance, men like Sidonius and Boethius. But most Romans the newcomers found to have none of these qualities. Most of them, it will not be too much to say, were beaten men before they ever saw a German warrior. To a *colonus* bound to the soil it made little difference that his master was now a barbarian and a foreigner. The things which mattered most, poverty and the loss of freedom, had entered his life before the Germans, and as for their barbarism, it would not have been easy for a Roman *colonus* to discern it in any but the most superficial ways. It is reasonable to assume that the defeatism which made of the old Roman population complacent victims of invasion also contributed to the quick and easy fusion of old and new institutions. So smooth and uneventful indeed was this fusion that it has left scarcely a trace.

The Beginnings of the New Society

What has here been described as a great social and economic revolution, namely the destruction of the middle class, the acquisition of many small landholdings by the great proprietors, and the resulting vast increase in the power of the landed aristocracy, was the basic feature of the transition from late Roman to medieval times, that is, from the more advanced but no longer workable imperial régime to the simpler but more practical régime of the landed lords.[91] The relationship of this change to the rise of the feudal system has been exaggerated or, better, distorted. No single "system" can be discerned in the forms of society and government prevailing in such areas as Italy, Christian Spain, France, England, and Germany beyond the Rhine.[92] Of large areas of medieval Spain it has been truly said that there was much feudalism but no feudal system.[93] As for England, we need only recall the protracted dispute over the character of "prefeudal" (i.e., pre-Conquest) English society, and the peculiar form of feudalism introduced by the Conqueror.[94] The common social denominator was not feudalism but the simple agrarian state of society resulting from the fall of Rome and the destruction of the middle class.

There were, of course, other dissimilarities between regions. Local differences in land and climate played their part, as did the power of Church and ruler, the time and nature of invasions, the relatively strong or weak survival of towns and contact with the East, and such local conditions as the warfare between Christian and Moslem in Spain. Only in the importance of land and land tenure, and in the close connection of administrative authority with the land, were all regions economically alike. It is on this account that feudalism should be rejected as the decisive element in the formation of medieval society. Important though it was, it was but one of several oligarchic devices in use in medieval Europe. In short, feudalism did not make possible a dominantly agricultural society, relatively poor and simple, loosely knit, and highly experimental in its approach to its problems. It was the decline of Rome that brought that society into being, and feudalism, far from being its cause and central principle, was but one result of its experiments.

Western Christianity, though more widespread than feudalism, was broadly analogous to it in origin. It was, as already noted, a new Christianity, or rather a Christianity with a new orientation, essentially original and quite distinct from that of the old Roman or the contemporary Byzantine civilizations. What gave Christianity the peculiarly powerful form and influence it assumed in Western Europe, as contrasted with the Byzantine Empire or Russia, was the nature of the Western society with which it grew up: poor, simple, agrarian, relatively free of binding tradition and intensely empirical. Aside from the almost indefinable character of the Western European peoples who created it, the *sine qua non* of the new civilization was its reduction to an agrarian level.

There were corresponding differences between early medieval Western and Eastern methods of government in the fourth and fifth centuries.[95] Here we must remember the poverty of the West and the relatively stable and prosperous economy of the East. Even when territorially restricted and plagued by almost constant attacks by foreign enemies, the East was able to maintain an effective bureaucracy, a small but well-equipped army and navy, and a steady and uniformly organized and operated financial system. This stability obviously was very important; for a thousand years, despite all temporary stresses and strains, faults, and reverses, it enabled the Byzantine state to act quickly and directly in crises. In this society the Church occupied an important but dependent position as an integral part of the State system. It was "in, not beside" the State, and its hierarchy functioned only as a part of the State's bureaucratic organization, which reached everywhere.[96]

This state of affairs presents a marked contrast with that of the West, where the fifth century merely witnessed the continuation, at a more rapid rate, of the decay that had been clear enough in the third and fourth. Naturally this deterioration did not proceed at the same speed throughout all regions of the West. In the Italy of Odovacar and Theodoric, for example, the old system, including the bureaucracy, remained largely in effect until the advent of the Lombards, who substituted a government by landowning princes who were supported by the produce of their land and contributed military service to the State as a personal obligation. In Gaul, also, much that was Roman lingered on, well into Frankish times. More of the Roman tax system survived among the Franks, for example, than among the Lombards; and in Frankish Gaul the hated direct land tax was easier to collect in the more Roman parts, more difficult in the German regions.[97]

The importance of the fact that these new states were based upon the ownership of land is inescapable. Whether one calls their economy a natural economy or not seems unimportant.[98] What matters is that it was an economy based on self-sufficient communities.[99] The bulk of the population lived in a semi-free status directly on the land, and their lords, the military branch of this simple society, were supported by what the peasantry produced. Was this a reappearance of the old type of society described by Aristotle, characterized by a division of labor between the working or productive and the fighting or protective class?[100] To a large degree it was. Admittedly, the early medieval society came immediately after a much more advanced society, which even in its failure and decay was capable of contributing a great deal to its successor; admittedly, there was no question of returning to the crude state of the earliest Greek *polis*. But this difference can be exaggerated; significant though Roman survivals were, they were only survivals, borrowings, and nothing more. The Western European civilization of the Middle Ages and after would have been essentially the same without them.

The effects of large landownership were very different in the East. Because of the relative stability of the Eastern economy, the survival of the urban middle class, and the revenues in money which they provided, the State was able to hold the proprietors in check, if not to do away with them. The great landowners were unable to swallow up the small holdings of the peasants and thereby to achieve independence from the central authority. This potentially feudal class retained considerable power and at times caused trouble, but it was prevented from breaking down and dividing up the administrative authority of the State.[101]

In the West, by contrast, the very distinction between public wealth belonging to the state and private treasure belonging to the king was soon lost. It could not have been otherwise in a self-sufficient, land-based economy. The paramount importance of ownership or control of land affected all subsequent developments, civil, military, and ecclesiastical. The feudal practice of granting the use of land in return for military service, for example, was a natural outgrowth of the new distribution of land. It is of secondary importance that other arrangements were possible: obviously, the course of development from patronage and *comitatus* through intermediate stages of military service and benefice eventually to the personal bond of vassalage and the clearly military benefice or fief varied from place to place and from time to time.

To sum up, the Middle Ages began not when full-fledged feudalism or something like it put in an appearance but long before with the political, economic, and social changes which in some lands eventually led to feudalism. In Rostovtzeff's words, "What happened was a slow and gradual change, a shifting of values in the consciousness of men."[102] Politically, the Roman Empire ceased to function effectively in the West when the imperial government could no longer curb the growing power of the *potentiores*. Economically, the Western Empire failed when commerce and industry could no longer be carried on profitably, even when commanded to do so, and when the middle class was hounded out of existence and the peasantry reduced to a dependent status. Socially, the end came when men of Roman birth and free ancestry faced a choice between serfdom and emigration. Eventually it all amounted to the same thing—life on a landed estate under the domination of a local lord. As for the date of these changes, the imperial government's strenuous efforts to control the *potentiores* had clearly failed before the end of the fourth century. We may assume that economically and socially the change was also well advanced before the end of this century, and for the same reasons; there is no other way of explaining the military defenselessness of the West and its feeble reliance upon barbarian troops.[103] Though Orosius and Salvian wrote in the fifth century, it is clear that what they described had begun long before.

It was inevitable that in this gradual but irresistible process of change standards and values should also alter. The majority of men who lived in the Late Roman Empire and the Early Middle Ages no longer regarded as vital what had seemed all-important to their predecessors. "They had their own notion of what was important, and most of what was essential in the classical period among the constituent parts of ancient civilization was discarded by them as futile and often detrimental."[104] The truth of Rostovtzeff's words is self-evident; yet to Western man since the Renaissance, the historian as well as the philosopher, the artist, and the scientist, it has been all but unpalatable. Blinded by our prejudice in favor of classical "civilization" as contrasted with medieval "barbarism," we have grossly misinterpreted the creative character of what was taking place in late Roman and early medieval times. We have confused adjustment with decay, and failing to recognize what may be called a change of pace and direction, we have branded it as exclusively an ending.

The shifting of values from standards set up under different conditions was made by men who had to cope with the realities of Western Europe in the fourth and fifth centuries. What may seem today to have been quite simply retrogression and nothing else, may from another point of view be regarded as a cutting away of dead wood. Early medieval man was confronted not with free and unlimited choices but with strictly limited opportunities, and it was from these opportunities that he had to choose. It is not likely that those who entered into a life of serfdom thought it was preferable to a life of freedom; indeed they could scarcely think of it in comparative terms, and it is more than likely that many of them did not think about it at all. They did not catch up with the times; the times caught up with them. In the social sphere, broadly conceived, men bade farewell, either wittingly or unwittingly, to the greater freedom, prosperity, and complexity of civilization known to some of their predecessors, and entered a state of subservience to overlords who owned or controlled vast estates by virtue of their military power.

Degradation, yes; but the end result over a very long period of time was not degradation. If the dead wood had not been cut away, efforts and experiments aiming at a more satisfying solution of the social problem of mankind than that worked out by the Roman Empire would have been impossible. One by one, experimentally, the military, the Church, much later the bourgeois, still later the workers, carved out an honorable place for themselves in the social structure. Had these experiments not started when they did, it seems safe to say, the cause of human freedom and dignity would have been greatly retarded. A thousand years of Byzantium produced extinction; a thousand years of medieval effort produced the Renaissance, the modern state, and ultimately the free world.

FOUR

The Medieval Metamorphosis:
Aspects of a Changing World

If Julius Caesar or Hadrian, both of whom traveled widely in the civilized world of their respective times, could have visited the Empire of the fifth or sixth century, they would have found many puzzling alterations in the external appearance of the world they had known. These changes, marked enough in the East, in the West would have been even more obvious, especially in such respects as the state of cities and towns, the make-up and disposition of the armies, the character of transportation and commerce, the daily occupations, and even the dress of the people.

Both visitors would no doubt have regarded the later Roman West as sadly down at heel. Still they would have recognized it. Though Caesar would doubtless have been disgusted at the state of Roman arms and Hadrian disheartened at the fate of his great cities, the "deterioration" they would have found would at least have been the deterioration of a more or less familiar set of visible and tangible Roman creations and practices. Much more startling would have been the discovery, if they had been capable of making it, that great though they found the external changes to be, they were minor compared with certain more subtle alterations in outlook, in values, in modes of thought, and in aspirations. The political, economic, and social developments considered in the last chapter were movements *away from* earlier Roman practices but still recognizable in terms of the age-old institutions in which they had originated. The other changes represented a movement *toward* something new and quite outside the experience of a Caesar or a Hadrian, and they were soon to be expressed in outward behavior as well as in thought and feeling.

The buildings, streets, theaters, and engineering works of a great city do not always disappear when those capable of planning and making them are no more. An emperor's tomb may endure to serve centuries later as a papal palace and a palazzo may remain as a tenement house. Still, there are changes: washing is strung out the tenement windows; minarets are added to Hagia Sophia. Changes in the realm of thought are less easy to apprehend. The real meaning of such an institution as an army, or a system of political administration, may undergo a vital transformation without revealing it through adjustments in name and aspect. In such circumstances an apparently vigorous social organization, a religion, for instance, or a tax system, may become a mere husk or shell without betraying, outwardly, the profound alteration it has suffered.

It is a function of historical study to interpret the whole change, specifically to keep the inner meaning abreast of the external appearance. It scarcely needs saying that this is not always easy to do. As we have seen, Syrian wine was shipped to France in the second century and also in the sixth. The product was the same, the means of transportation the same, the source and destination the same: what is more likely than that the circumstances were the same, that the prevailing conditions in the Mediterranean were the same? History cannot be written without analogies of this sort, based on facts of this order. And yet in such an interpretation the historian may be failing to recognize new developments of unfamiliar aspect; he may be passing over wheat to busy himself with chaff. He may be describing a husk from the outside, leaving the impression that it is more than a husk.

It is the purpose of this chapter to examine four different aspects of the new world taking shape behind, and partly obscured by, the mantle of the old. The epoch-making change or series of changes going on between the fourth and fifth and the ninth and tenth centuries took place both inwardly and outwardly, (1) in the way men thought and in what they thought about, (2) in the way they lived and expressed themselves, (3) in what they thought worth doing, and (4) in how they did it. What was actually happening in this period—i.e., what men were doing and what they were thinking that prompted them to do it—was very different from what actually happened in the days of Roman power. There are several reasons for considering these particular four fields of thought and action here: they did not become important or even exist before the fourth century; they operated for some time alongside the types of changing Roman institutions and ways of thought considered in the last chapter; they were essential to the formation of the distinctively medieval civilization.

It must be stressed that the changes in these four fields began before and continued after the period A.D. 650–750, to which Pirenne assigns the great change from the "secular" world of antiquity to the localized, rural, and "ecclesiastical" world of the Middle Ages; and that by 650 not even the outward manifestations of thought, except in the most superficial ways, remind one of the Greco-Roman world of antiquity.

It is of course true that the objects, methods, and values of intellectual life were changing before the time of Constantine, and that other elements of the medieval scene were by no means new: Christian missionary activity of a kind had begun long before; the seigniorial system had antecedents in the pre-Roman past; technology, both in the Orient and in the Greco-Roman West, had made notable advances in ancient times. What is different and historically significant is that these activities, and others, now appeared in the West together, operating and affecting each other as they had, and have, nowhere else and at no other time. This is what is meant by the assertion that they had not existed before the fourth century, specifically that they had not existed together and in such circumstances. All civilizations borrow from the past. When two civilizations borrow from the same past, the distinction between them arises not simply from what was borrowed but from the unique concatenation of borrowed, borrowers, and the circumstances of the borrowing. For example, the medieval West learned much from Greek philosophy, as did the Roman and Byzantine civilizations; yet in each case what was learned differed because of the borrowers and the circumstances of the borrowing. Similarly, as we have seen above, the Christian religion in the medieval West was not what it had been in Rome or became in Byzantium.

The primary thesis of this chapter, therefore, and indeed of this work as a whole, is that something new, distinct, and essentially original began in the Western European portion of the Roman Empire; that its elements are distinguishable by the fourth century, and some of them earlier. This "something" is perhaps best described as a new attitude toward life. In the centuries of its formation, this attitude is partly obscured by the more familiar and eye-catching externalities of Roman survival, by the turbulence of the time, and by the scarcity of our sources. Much of the information we should most like to have did not strike contemporaries as worthy of preservation in any form; some has been lost to us in other ways, by fires, wars, and careless handling. Perhaps the worst menace of all has been certain powerful *idées fixes*: the preoccupation with the vast epic of the decline and fall; the "authoritative" conviction that the early Middle Ages were a time of superstitious ignorance and general lethargy, enlivened only by fitful flashes of barbaric violence and cruelty. The imperceptive but unforgettable image of "vultures feeding on the carrion" and "maggots crawling in the carcass," conjured up by Toynbee, may be mentioned in passing.[1]

We know now that the Dark Age was not that dark. Ignorance, lethargy, and disorder existed then as now, but they were far from blighting an age eager for learning, vigorous in living and in expressing itself, and idealistically constructive. Perhaps it is not too much to say that medieval society was functional in ways not even dreamed of by antiquity and leading to ends beyond the imagination of earlier times. By "functional" I mean that it was a working, striving society, impelled to pioneer, forced to experiment, often making mistakes but also drawing upon the energies of its people much more fully than its predecessors, and eventually allowing them much fuller and freer scope for development. That conditions, events, and peoples came together as they did in the early Middle Ages was extremely fortunate for the present heirs of the Western tradition. What happened and why was it fortunate? In this chapter I shall endeavor to answer both questions.

I cannot go on to this final task, however, without first specifically acknowledging my debt to the brilliant and clear-sighted students whose research and wisdom have done so much to illuminate this era, above all to Marc Bloch and Lefebvre des Noëttes. Without them even the brief and tentative interpretation essayed here would have been impossible.

Changing Moods of Thought and Expression

It has long been recognized that the Church, to its own profit and that of the whole West, borrowed much from the organization of the Roman State, with such modifications as were necessary to meet the needs of a new institution operating in different conditions, performing new as well as old functions, and serving ends unheard of in the great days of Roman power. Thanks to the influence of the Church in every branch of aesthetic and intellectual endeavor, much of the order and system of Roman thought penetrated to where it could best be used. And yet in the new art of the Late Roman era and in the still newer art brought in by the barbarians there was much that was vigorous and original, much that owed nothing to Rome, that derived its inspiration solely from the new needs and values of the emerging medieval world. Nothing better attests the creative genius, the capacity both to learn and to originate, of Western European civilization, even in the period of its youth, than the mighty products of its religious art, which combined spiritual aspiration, warm human feeling, and artistic excellence in a way unknown to pagan, classical antiquity.[2]

As it was with art, so it was with social and intellectual standards, and indeed with the very modes of thought. The intellectual life of the new world of the Middle Ages was cast in a mold essentially different from that of classical—chiefly Hellenic—antiquity. One of the great turning points in the history of thought came when the Greeks began not merely to acquire knowledge, which had been done before, but to speculate about it, to unite science and philosophy. The legacy of this union has never been exhausted, though the Romans could not wholly appreciate it and since the beginning of the Middle Ages Western European men have sometimes seen fit to use the income in ways that would doubtless seem strange to the founders of the fortune.

In the Late Empire the Hellenic fires burned dimly. Science lost vitality and the old union with philosophy was dissolved. There were new needs to be met; it served no better now for intellectuals to recall the glories of the Academy than for Salvian's dispossessed farmers to think on the grandeur of the Roman name and the freedom of their ancestors. Philosophy contracted a new alliance, this time with theology; henceforth for some centuries intellectual life was to proceed under the guidance of the Church. The learning of the past was in part kept and transformed, in part virtually ignored. Christian leaders, above all St. Augustine, strove with energy and success to reorganize the patterns of thought and to adapt such classical knowledge and intellectual endeavors as were retained to the new goals of human life, a life in which salvation had become the main concern of educated men.[3]

St. Augustine is rightly given the place of prominence. Of all the tasks imposed upon the human intellect perhaps the most difficult is first to perceive in times of vast fundamental change what is dead and spiritless and devoid of meaning, and then to conceive, perfect, and propagate values more suitable to the new age. Most men in all ages, and very likely more in times of turmoil than in times of stability, cling staunchly and blindly to the familiar and accepted, avoiding the cold discomfort of mental and spiritual readjustment. In recognizing what was dead or dying, and in giving meaning to what was living and being born, St. Augustine has had few equals.[4] The *Confessions* and the *City of God* alone tell us how power-ful for him was the appeal of the past. His mastery lay in the recognition that for his own and future generations, in the conditions of life as they had come to be, the voices of Plato and the rest were but echoes from a tomb. He did not repudiate what he had borrowed from Plato; he used it. But he selected only what he considered valuable, adapted it to new conditions, and made it part of an intellectual structure that would have been incom-prehensible to the Academy.

It is proper to ask of history whether there is any valid reason for assuming that human genius flamed less brightly when men, for good reasons of their own and of their age, deflected speculative thought from science-philosophy to theology-philosophy. Presumably the men of the Late Empire and the early Middle Ages were born with as much capacity for thought, inquiry, and intellectual growth as the men of any other age. The question, then, is not whether they had ability but whether they would or could use it, and how they would choose to use it. Here a distinction must be made between the late classical and the early medieval attitude, as noted in the discussion of Pirenne's views on the decadence of classical culture.

There is discernible before the fourth century not a universal but a wide-spread decline in the quality of the intellectual and literary works belonging to the classical tradition. That tradition had lost a great deal of its vitality, and its followers seemed no longer convinced that the subjects with which they dealt were meaningful. The thinkers and writers of the Patristic tra-dition, by contrast, had complete faith in the urgency of what concerned them and wrote about it with energy and assurance, in apologetics, in exegesis, in homiletics, in works on ecclesiastical organization and super-vision, on asceticism and hagiography, on the doctrinal controversies. It is generally the assumption of our age that these productions, particularly the last, represent wasted time. This is not the opinion, however, of those who know them well and recognize the place they hold in the development of the thought processes of Western man. Many of the controversies were dreary and futile affairs; many of the controversialists were inspired by economic and political motives or by personal interest, and wrote more passionately than intelligently. It remains true that the theological disputes very often dealt with subjects of undying concern to mankind, that fre-quently they were waged with sincerity and brilliance, and that they gave a strong impetus to the development of a method of thought keen, probing, and logical. Their contribution to the formation in later centuries of scholastic philosophy, one of the high points in the development of Western thought, is sufficiently well known to require no description here.

Thus we must be extremely cautious in passing judgment upon the intellectual accomplishments of the Patristic Age in comparison with those of classical antiquity. Divergence from the earlier standard we must recognize, simplification and even abandonment in some areas of learning we must acknowledge, but to issue a general condemnation of the intellectual life of the age as decadent, retrogressive, and benighted is simply to open the way to hopeless distortion of the historical realities and to make it impossible to understand them. There can be no denying that such evils as poverty, instability, and violence became worse after the time of St. Jerome and St. Augustine before they became better, and that intellectual pursuits suffered along with everything else. The essential consideration is that by the fourth century a new intellectual attitude toward the world had been well launched; that this attitude was not necessarily either superior or inferior to that of classical antiquity, but simply different; and that the circumstances and nature of its development were of the greatest consequence. It is doubtful that any attitude of mind and spirit less toughly welded, less aggressive, and less convinced of its mission could have weathered the storms that were to envelop Western Europe in the centuries ahead.

Remarkably enough, some at least of the intellectual leaders among the Christian clergy were aware that something very crucial, something requiring explanation, was taking place. They were not certain just what was happening, nor did they always know how to explain it, but such startling events as the capture of the city of Rome by Alaric and his Visigoths raised questions that demanded answers. Some Christians who were well versed in the speculations of the classical philosophers offered cyclical theories. Others spoke of the Millennium.[5]

Many Christian apologists felt it necessary to try to explain away the continuance of calamities after the beginning of the Christian era, which may be taken as a testimony both to their devotion to the old, long-established materialistic attitude toward the world and to their intellectual naïveté. When Constantine had begun to favor the new religion, the Christians of his time had been swept by a wave of optimism and assurance that material conditions would soon improve. Eusebius and other writers after him were quick to link the material welfare of the Empire and its steady improvement with the victory of Christianity.[6] This attitude is strikingly and rather pathetically exemplified in Prudentius's invective against Symmachus, written after Pollentia, which the poet obviously regarded as a great Roman victory, and before Alaric's capture and sack of Rome.[7] To attribute the success of Roman arms so confidently to Christianity was to run the risk of great future embarrassment. Once the connection was made, Roman defeats were bound to increase the derision of the pagans and cause bitter soul-searching on the part of thoughtful Christians.

We have already noted that Orosius and Salvian were aware that profound changes were in the making. The former, though no great intellect, at least saw the necessity of answering the pagan charge that desertion of the old gods had deprived Rome of their protection.[8] This man, moreover, who could make the famous remark "ubique patria, ubique lex et religio mea est" (*Historiarum adversum paganos libri vii,* V, 2, 1) and add that he was "inter Romanos . . . Romanus, inter Christianos Christianus, inter homines homo" (V, 2, 6), saw no little good in the barbarians and had hopes that Romans and Germans might live peacefully side by side (VII, 41, 7). He was also conscious of what Roman supremacy had cost and strongly suggested that the fall of the Empire, though unfortunate for the Romans, was justified because of the great benefits it brought to many others (V, 1, 4; VII, 41, 8).[9] Later in the fifth century Salvian, too, though giving the Romans up as hopelessly damned, saw much to admire in the Germans.

It remained for Augustine of Hippo, however, to accept the challenge of his time on the highest intellectual plane and state the case for the rising Christian culture in his powerful philosophy of history.[10] He saw that it was necessary not only to reply to the gibes of the pagans, but also to scotch the popular identification of the welfare of Christianity with the welfare of Rome. Though he doubtless thought of the problem primarily and immediately as one of apology, he was unquestionably aware that the whole meaning of history for Christians was also involved. He broke with certain contemporary and earlier historical theories and set about disabusing Christian minds of the expectation of steady material progress. Ultimately he rejected the concept of the materialistic progress of the earthly city for all future ages, and for his own time he cut the tie binding together the fates of the Christian religion and the Roman State. It is particularly interesting in our own age to note that Augustine did not ignore the inventions made by human genius and the practical advances made by human industry; as Theodor Mommsen has recently pointed out, he was also aware that the inventions included new poisons, new weapons and machines of destruction.[11] Few men have better understood the nature of the world. His recognition that Christianity must be cut loose from the Roman State was not timeserving; naturally in his philosophy of history the *civitas dei* would always be independent of the destinies of worldly states.

Did Augustine fully understand that he was helping prepare the road which the new world of the future would follow as it departed from the crumbling ruins of the Roman Empire and the classical past?[12] So much could be expected of no man. Like Orosius, Augustine had reservations about some of Rome's accomplishments, but he still hoped the Empire would stand. He was not omniscient. His accomplishment was to prepare the minds of his more thoughtful contemporaries and successors for the possibility of a change in the political state of affairs as they knew it, and to enable them to adapt themselves to this change.[13] He was a pioneer on the frontiers of thought; like all pioneers, he pushed into vast unknown areas, made his way as best he could, and did not always fully take in all he saw from mountaintops. He blazed new trails; others followed them, widened them, pushed them further.

St. Augustine, though perhaps the greatest intellectual leader of the new age in terms of ability and influence, was not the only one. His contributions in theology, education, and monastic development were matched and sometimes bettered by other thinkers and Fathers of the Church, among them St. Jerome, Leo the Great, Boethius, Cassiodorus, and Gregory the Great. As for influence alone, if only one other leader besides Augustine could be named, it would be a man whose intellectual output is in no way comparable with his, for it could be none other than Benedict of Nursia, the legislator of Western monasticism. Augustine produced an ideology. St. Benedict, setting out, as he put it, to wage war against the Devil, provided the model of an active way of religious life.

Others there were in great numbers, Orientals, Greeks, Celts, and Germans, who invented new and adapted foreign forms of art, learning, and science, as they were found needful and available in the constantly changing new world of the West. Many of their works, especially some of their literary products, seem pitiably naïve and useless now, which is the chief reason why their era is called a Dark Age.

To repeat, this terminology "Dark Age" is based on fallacious reasoning. One might equally well conclude, after a comparative study of classical Greek and contemporary American engineering accomplishments, that the Greeks scarcely deserve to be called civilized. It is much closer to the truth to say that the creative genius of early medieval men did not lie, or was not to be exercised, in literary learning of the old classical type. It was to express itself in other ways and to operate under the aegis of different aims and values. If comparisons must be made, these new forms must be reckoned with. It was not, after all, merely by chance that the towns, societies, arts, and crafts of a later and more advanced Europe were quite different from those of the Greeks and the Romans. They became so because they headed in a decidedly different direction from the time of their origin in the long age of Western European disruption and slow regeneration.

The Pioneer Society: Missionary Monks and the Winning of the West for Christianity

The foregoing description of St. Augustine as a cultural pioneer reintroduces a theme already briefly mentioned but to be stressed in the concluding sections of this interpretation; it is that in many respects the beginning of the Middle Ages was a pioneering movement. The pioneering is not the sort Americans are most familiar with; more than time alone separates St. Augustine from Daniel Boone. Frontiers need not always be geographical, and the relationship of the old to the new is not invariably, as in more recent times, that of a vigorous, relatively rich, technically much superior culture to one numerically weak, economically poor, and technically backward. Nonetheless, in Europe from sixteen to thirteen centuries ago, much as in America in the last century, there were wildernesses and savages to contend with and a new way of life to create.

Although the expansion was guided and supported by a Church which had its administrative and cultural capital in Italy, the oldest and strongest center of culture in the West, the molders and bearers of the rising civilization had to rely mainly upon their own resources. Consequently what emerged was not simply the result of the transmission of a culture but the product of this transmission in the peculiar conditions of life found in semi-barbarous and materially backward northern and western European communities. To make possible a society in which paramount importance attached to individualism, to adjustment and adaptation, to experimentation and invention, and to a new standard of human values, it seems safe to say that the clash and fusion of classical, Germanic, and Celtic tastes, traditions, and cultures in something resembling a frontier environment and under the spiritual guidance of the Christian Church was necessary.

In the foregoing pages the significance of the simplicity, poverty, and lack of established order in the initial stages of the new Western European civilization has been repeatedly emphasized. The point can be illustrated by a closer look at some of the major conditions and movements of the age.

Such an attempt to see good in conditions of poverty, disorder, and cultural retrogression clearly runs counter to the conventional approach in historical interpretation. The commonly accepted view has long been that, with the decline in the vital forces of the Roman Empire and the classical civilization which it supported, the course of history entered upon a long, grim period of breakdown and futility. Though few would now with Gibbon regard Byzantine history as "a tedious and uniform tale of weakness and misery," still the Eastern Roman civilization is generally considered decadent or at best static.[14] The West, degraded by barbarism and enslaved by superstition, is seen as simply marking time until the Renaissance. Thus the Middle Ages, in both East and West, has remained, even for most students of history aside from medievalists, simply the period between decline and rebirth. It has been one of the principal aims of the present essay to show that, in the light of what we have learned from recent research, re-examination of long-accepted views, and new interpretations of the evidence, the old conception of the Middle Ages is no longer tenable. Rostovtzeff expressed it well when he insisted that in the formula "decay of ancient civilization" the stress must be laid upon "ancient" and not upon "civilization."[15]

All the old views—the Renaissance aesthetic contempt, the Enlightenment's anticlerical sneers, the economic snobbery of the early twentieth century—are still alive. All are the products of ignorance and bias, the more surprising because the proponents of these views abhorred those evils and thought they were free of them. All are primarily negative. All are quite wrong.

During the chaotic age in which the Western tradition was born, new knowledge was only partly acquired in schools. The schools maintained

by the Church, chiefly in monasteries, were repositories of the old knowledge, much of it meaningless to early medieval men; by necessity they were
to some extent experimental in what they taught. Most of what men of this
period learned, however, they learned directly, like men on all frontiers
and in all times of turmoil, from the experience of living. As new needs
arose they were met on the spot as well as could be, just as they still are
today in industry. Doubtless also successful solutions suggested ideas for
new needs and additional improvements.

The social revolution discussed in the previous chapter must be kept
in mind when we think of what happened in Western Europe in the period
of conversion and the expansion of Christianity. It could not but be important that, as Orosius and Salvian tell us, in the fifth century in vast areas
of the West the old Celtic and Roman population was becoming fused, not
only socially but also economically, with the Germanic newcomers. It seems
likely that of the two dichotomies, Roman-German (or Roman-barbarian)
and Christian-pagan, even with much allowance made for "old Roman"
snobbery, the Christian-pagan was already the more important in the fifth
century.

For all the importance of the new art and literature and of the social
revolution, however, our best single illustration of the new way of life is
afforded by the monastic expansion. When most of Western Europe, the
once civilized as well as the uncivilized portions, took on the character of
an agrarian society, it obviously became impossible for the old modes of
propagating culture through urban centers to continue to operate. The
State—i.e., the barbarian government—could not perform the task. The
Church, which was in some respects more powerful than the State and in
all respects better organized, could. The relationship between the two had
been foreshadowed by St. Augustine in the *City of God*; according to this
view, the Church as the representative of the eternal city was the superior,
the State a subordinate partner. The Church, or rather its hierarchy of
bishops, was both able to take an active part in secular affairs and willing
to run the risk of being made worldly itself. No secular work harmonized
better with its desires and capacities than the work of promoting Christian
culture.

In the conditions of the time there was only one way of extending knowledge and building a new culture, and that was by sending agents out to
live and work in the agrarian communities under barbarian rule. These

agents were mainly monks, and the monastic centers they established—first among the predominantly pagan rural peoples of such Romanized regions as Gaul and then among the even less civilized barbarians, many of them beyond the bounds of the former Empire—were like outposts or fortresses in a hostile land.

At first we know but little of the work done by the monastic pioneers. Only a few of their names—St. Martin of Tours, John Cassian—have come down to us. In the sixth century, however, the monastic institution became steadily more vigorous and effective. Its efforts were greatly abetted by the organizing work of St. Benedict of Nursia and others, and infused with new zeal by the fiery recruits of Ireland and other remote Celtic regions. Then and thereafter the famous names of missionary monks found in medieval annals become more numerous, and we get a clearer picture of their accomplishments.

It is scarcely surprising that two centuries passed between the beginning of monasticism in Gaul and the great impetus given the movement there and elsewhere by the Irish missionaries. No less than the conversion and civilization of the whole of Western Europe was contemplated, and ultimately accomplished. An army of monks had to be recruited and trained; naturally the process was slow, especially in its initial stages.

Once the peasants of the Roman portions of the West had been turned into Christians, it was possible to look to new fields. Early in the seventh century, a second St. Augustine, at the head of a mission of Benedictine monks, effected the conversion of England and created a new center of Christian activity at Canterbury. Thence came the Anglo-Saxon monks, above all St. Boniface, who in the eighth century carried forward the process of converting and civilizing Germany. Behind the frontier, as it advanced, a great work of organization, of education, of the general raising of cultural levels, and of ecclesiastical reform constantly went on.

Gibbon erroneously describes these early monasteries as refuges, chiefly inhabited by fainthearted men of aesthetic and intellectual inclinations, by idlers and wasters looking for an easy life, and by others who were unwilling or afraid to face the world. The monastic life did attract some men of this type, as St. Benedict frankly remarks at the beginning of his *Rule,* and there were others, even in the West, whose strongly ascetic bent made them unfit to participate in the cooperative and constructive work of cenobitic life. Most, however, were active and courageous; it was these who worked among the Franks and other early invaders, faced the hostile Lombards in Italy, went to Ireland, Scotland, England, Iceland, Germany, and the Scandinavian countries. They were sane and hardheaded men; they faced facts. Turning their backs on the solitary life of prayer, often no doubt with reluctance, they did the work which they alone were able to do.

The elements of the problem were clear. A relatively small number of men had to reach a great many, widely scattered in rural communities, and from the monastic centers of worship and instruction give visible proof of the superiority of their way of life. Thus it was—and it must have been so from the first, though we have more detailed information beginning with the Merovingian era—that the pioneer monks lived with the peasants and shared their labors in plowing and planting, in reclaiming land, and in clearing away forests.[16] The work of Boniface (d. 754) and his followers must have been more dangerous than that of the earlier Gallic, Italian, and Irish missionaries of the Merovingian age, but very likely, in the absence of Roman remains, it provided even greater opportunities for demonstrating the superiority of the Christian culture and religion. When a party of missionaries moved into a new region, in some cases with an excellent boat, and began to clear land, to erect buildings (sometimes of stone), to plant a vineyard or divert a stream to their use, to construct a mill, or to do intricate work in metal, the pagans must have been deeply impressed.[17] The missionaries were seen to be much more than preachers of a new religion; they were teachers, builders, physicians, metalworkers—above all, perhaps, they were farmers, like the people among whom they lived.

In the East, where Christianity reached the rural regions from the beginning, there was no such difference between townspeople and peasantry as in the Roman West.[18] Moreover, the conversion of the Slavs and Byzantium's other pagan neighbors was strongly and effectively supported by the State; the way had been carefully prepared by political and economic pressure even before the missionaries appeared. As the emissary of a rich, powerful, highly organized government with all the resources of a subtle and complicated statecraft and all the persuasions of an advanced and efficient society at its disposal, the Eastern missionary usually had only to set the new religion before his intended converts; he acted before them only in his role of religious man.

The Western missionary could rely on no such support from the government and lay society. It is true that some Frankish rulers even of the Merovingian period gave assistance to the monks, but until the time of Charlemagne this assistance was irregular, and because of the weaknesses of the government and its inability to maintain its authority everywhere steadily, it was always unreliable.[19] Even with the stronger support supplied by Charlemagne and his successors, the cooperation between State and missionaries never reached the same degree of effectiveness as in the East. Such leaders as Boniface had to spend a considerable part of their own time and energy in trying to obtain the sort of support that was rendered automatically in the East. The pope and other high Church officials helped out where they could, but the task of converting the pagans and making them a part of the growing culture was accomplished largely by strong individual missionaries relying chiefly on their own resources.

Eastern and Western missionaries also differed in their presentation of the Christian religion. In the East the emphasis was on dogma and literary education. In the West missionaries had to adopt a much more practical approach: they made use of pagan temples and customs when possible, played up the material advantages of Christianity, and emphasized conduct and worship rather than doctrinal matters.[20] The Eastern method worked more rapidly, but the Western method worked better in the long run. It was essential for the development of the Western tradition as we know it that its beginnings should be slow and gradual, that it should be allowed freedom and time to find its own natural course, to meet its problems with self-reliance, and to discover its bent for positive and original construction, inquiry, and invention—in a word, that it should be allowed to grow independently rather than in the shadow of an already great neighbor, a neighbor with established patterns of culture to be had for the aping.

It is for this reason that I have made so much of the rugged character of the conditions under which the West began, the agrarian nature of its economy and of its social organization, the division and feebleness of its agencies of government, the imperviousness of its peoples to advanced literary education in the old tradition, and its reluctance to receive complicated theological instruction.[21] It is for this same reason that I have emphasized the frontier quality of the beginning of the Middle Ages, and the pioneer monks who were so much more than transmitters of a religion.

The part I have assigned to the Church in this cultural development is not in harmony with the still common emphasis on the work of the Church in literary education, philosophy, and theology. Religious men did of course supply almost all the literary education given in schools, but this was only one part of their contribution. As for the opposite view, that the Church cultivated superstition and ignorance, no greater distortion of the truth can be imagined. Some medieval ecclesiastics—like some men in all ages, on all continents, of all occupations—were bigoted, overzealous, self-seeking, ignorant, and inclined to take short cuts to what they considered good ends. To say that some men are not big enough for their responsibilities is not to say that all responsibility has been ignored or abdicated.

Superstition was indeed rife, but the prevalence of such states of mind depends primarily upon the cultural level and the general character of societies rather than upon one or another institution. Consider the old classical interest in science, which became moribund in the Late Roman Empire. Had its decline been due to systematic obscurantism on the part of the Church, we should confidently expect to find it snuffed out altogether, or at best preserving a furtive and clandestine existence. But as we shall soon see, science did not wholly die in the West, nor did it go underground. Like Western society in general, Western science was crude and concerned exclusively with agriculture. The conclusion seems clear: in form, nature, and achievement, early medieval science responded to the needs and capacities of an impoverished agrarian society, not to any institutional policy. The analogy with superstition should be obvious.

It is greatly to the credit of the Church that some of its agents were self-reliant men of character and vision. As Richard E. Sullivan has described it, in approaching the pagans, "The West presented the aspect of a growing civilization, one that needed yet to be built both in its material and in its spiritual and intellectual phases."[22] It was as collaborators, not as superiors and subordinates, that the men of the older and newer West created the European tradition. Despite all the disadvantages of this arrangement, and all the demoralizing and harassing aspects of their task, the conditions under which they worked can only be called ideal.

A Changing Society: The Seigniorial System

Are there other signs that in this impoverished agrarian world a new civilization and a new way of life were being brought into existence? The shadows are so thick, the obscurity so forbidding, that one may venture to say so only with great caution. Happily, the shadows have been in part dispelled by contemporary scholars, notably Marc Bloch, one of the most original and productive of the recent historians of medieval France. Bloch's sound scholarship and expert use of the technique of comparative history[23] have been especially useful in clarifying the rise of the seigniorial system.[24] There was considerable difference in the *seigneurie* in the various parts of Europe, even within areas we are today inclined to think of as unified by nature, but it is now possible nevertheless to make out the general line of movement. As Bloch has asked, ". . . in what science has the presence of variations or varieties ever interfered with the recognition of a genus?"[25]

In certain areas of economic activity there took place a reversion to simpler, pre-Roman conditions, and future progress—for progress there certainly was—went on from that state of affairs. This advancement, when it came, did not follow slavishly along the old Roman lines but sometimes struck off in quite different directions. The view is still strongly supported, however, that, save for a few exceptions, the transition from Roman to medieval agriculture meant the loss of much and the gain of very little.[26] Actually, although early medieval agricultural methods were at first in many respects far behind the most advanced Roman methods, in the long run the change was worth all it cost. Roman agriculture, despite all its contributions and achievements, had been following a blind alley; before new advances could be made, much of the way had to be retraced and a new beginning undertaken in simpler conditions.

Bloch has pointed out that it is not until the ninth century in Gaul, Italy, and the Rhineland, and even later in England, that we may form a distinct picture of the *seigneurie*. But in those regions the seigniorial system (or as we have long called it after the English usage, the manorial system) was then firmly established and was already a very old institution.[27] Certain of its features—the tithe, the land tax, the *mansus*—were centuries old; the *mansus*, for example, is attested in Italy from the beginning of the sixth century.[28] The clearing of wooded land went on throughout the Frankish period, long before the great work that began in the middle of the eleventh century.[29]

Of outstanding importance in the passage from Roman to medieval practice was the decline of slavery. Fewer slaves were acquired by war, and the Church staunchly opposed the enslavement of orthodox Christians. Most important of all, with the breakdown of the large-scale exchange-profit economy of earlier Roman times, which had required abundant capital, relatively stable conditions, and very careful supervision, including the keeping of accurate accounts, slaves became a burden.[30] "To adopt tenancy as a solution was the line of least resistance." Thereafter labor took care of itself; families had their own small pieces of land; and custom soon dictated the laborers' days of work on the lord's demesne, the *mansus indominicatus*.[31]

It is highly significant that the combining of tenure with service, though not unknown in the Late Empire, became widely established only after the invasions.[32] Bloch has pointed out that this evolutionary process was later reproduced "almost feature by feature" and for the same reasons, with feudal vassals, who progressed from a *comitatus* fed by their chieftain in his own hall to their new position as members of the feudal aristocracy, i.e., as vassals but enfeoffed and therefore also lords over their own *seigneuries*. In spite of the outstanding differences between tenants and vassals, "viewed from the economic angle, the positions of the two classes are fundamentally similar."[33]

It is not my purpose to follow Bloch's work in detail, since our concern here is primarily with the bearing of seigniorial origins on the beginning of the Western tradition. It is clear that the origins of the medieval *seigneurie* reach far back into history, into Roman times and even beyond to a dim era of rural chiefdoms. The passing centuries encrusted this core with successive layers of customs. In the Roman era there came the great demesnes, the *latifundia*, which employed large numbers of slaves and usually a scattering of dependent peasants. Beginning with the second century, changing economic, military, and religious conditions combined with the invasions to transform the slaves into tenants. In time the free *coloni* also became tenants, and they were soon indistinguishable (except by law) from servile tenants. Certain words (e.g., *servus*, which becomes *serf* in the Romance tongue) and legal expressions preserved the idea of slavery or servile origins, but in the actual customs of life this was a fiction.[34]

The conditions which led Romans to put themselves under the authority of men capable of protecting them equally afflicted the barbarian kingdoms. These feebly governed states had even less money, even fewer responsible officials, even worse means of communication, than the Late Empire. The only answer was further decentralization. The specific solution seems to have been stumbled upon rather than deliberately sought out or planned from above. Royal action—the granting of concessions, immunities, or gifts—simply recognized an existing state of affairs.[35] One thing led to another: for example, where the head of the *seigneurie* at first had only the duty of requiring men under his control to appear in court, he ultimately took over the royal right of *ban*, the right to judge, command, and punish. Having thus greatly strengthened their own power at the expense of royal authority, the lords extended it as they could beyond the original immune territory, and used it to exact dues of various kinds from those subject to their will.[36]

For obvious reasons the feudal and seigniorial systems advanced together. Where allodial, or free, holdings were more numerous, as in England, both systems were weaker and customs were looser and more varied.[37] After the invasions the movement toward dependency in holdings where tenancy was combined with services proceeded more rapidly, along with the movement from the *comitatus* to the lord and vassal relationship of feudalism. Despite the fact that the homage of a vassal and the subordination of a humble man were originally related (by the practice of commendation), the two classes became widely separated.[38] Once the peasant was taken under the protection of a lord, he was made to pay as much in the way of dues and services as possible. Unless he could obtain redress at once, which was very difficult to do, he was only too likely to find himself permanently victimized. What started out as an abuse became a custom and eventually was claimed as a right.[39] In the course of the Middle Ages the seigniorial system came to be the means of subsistence of the nobler classes, who shaped it to serve their purposes as the occasion permitted.

Although the transition from large slave gangs on the *latifundia* to servile tenure on *seigneuries* is reasonably easy to follow, the relationship between the Late Roman colonate and seigniorial tenure presents a thornier problem. Superficially so similar, the two institutions were yet essentially different. What was the line of connection between them? How is the chronological progression from colonate to seigniorial status to be explained? Bloch offers the best answer: "The system of the colonate is only intelligible if we suppose that there existed before it a sort of embryo *seigneurie*."[40]

Where there was no such *seigneurie*, notably in the papal Campagna, conditions remained close to what they had been on the *latifundia* of antiquity. The peasants were not protected by the customs that grew up in seigniorial communities; they had few rights and many burdens; they were harshly exploited and lived in a condition very close to slavery. There was virtually no improvement, even in methods of farming. The peasant's life was endless drudgery; it has rightly been described as the most deadening and inhumane in medieval annals. There was apparently less change from ancient to medieval in the papal Campagna than anywhere else in Europe. "Instead of coming up from serfdom, as many of the peasantry of Europe elsewhere did, the Roman peasant went down, or rather never rose above the condition of his forebears in the fifth and sixth centuries."[41] As we know, the economic history of much of medieval Italy differed from that of most of Europe in a number of ways.[42] Still it is clear that where the seigniorial institution was free to grow, the condition of the peasantry tended to improve, whereas in the Campagna the reverse was true.

The original cell of the *mansus* appears to have been the patriarchal family and its holdings, to judge from what we know of the taxing unit officially called *iugum* or *caput*.[43] This unit corresponded to the *mansus* or hide, originally the landholding of one family (taken in the patriarchal sense rather than in the modern), which the Franks and Anglo-Saxons used as the tax unit. It is very likely that this system of land division, which was paralleled elsewhere under different names, e.g., *hufe* in Germany, *bol* in Denmark, was simply taken over by Roman tax experts for the excellent reason that it was already established.[44]

The significance of this discovery of Bloch's is tremendous; among other things it means no less than that a device long hailed as one of the most important of Roman survivals into the Frankish period had actually been borrowed by the Romans in the first place and already had centuries of history behind it. Another striking evidence of the antiquity and hardiness of the embryo *seigneurie* is the persistence in customs of the relationship between chief and lesser men and the continuation of the customs of the village community as a social force. The peasant owed certain things, gifts, to the chief, but he also had certain obligations—in such vital matters as grazing and rotation of crops—to the social group, the village, in which he lived. These obligations were all sternly maintained by custom, and since the society was collective, these customary obligations affected the chief or lord as well as the peasants. The relationship of gifts and customs to seigniorial dues and services is clear.[45] Still another impressive parallel is found in the remote division between chief and dependent peasants and the medieval cleavage between nobles and villagers.[46] In effect, the new trend simply continued a development that for some centuries had been halted, or directed into different channels, by Roman domination.

Socially and economically, then, the reverse revolution of the fourth and fifth centuries prepared the way for the beginning of the Middle Ages. In some fields of activity, e.g., the decline of slavery, the process was under way well before that time. In other areas the movement was slower; there were still townsmen in the time of Gregory of Tours, some elements of Roman law and administration hung on, and the reforming emperors may even be said to have halted the decline for a time here and there, as in certain aspects of public finance. Yet the general trend was downward toward poverty, decentralization, and disorganization.

Is it paradoxical to maintain, as I have done, that this was not wholly disastrous, that the failure and destruction of Roman institutions meant more than a return to barbarism, from which Europe would have to fight its way back once more slowly and with dreadful pain to what it had formerly enjoyed under Roman leadership? Beyond doubt there was violence and destruction. Towns were captured and sometimes burned, their inhabitants were mistreated and sometimes murdered, women were outraged, religious houses as well as the country estates of wealthy Romans were sacked and given to the flames, agriculture suffered heavily as did commerce, much property changed hands and many slaves and peasants changed masters. The Visigoths distinguished themselves as destroyers in the old Greek lands before capturing the city of Rome, and the Alemanni, Vandals, Huns, and Lombards did the same, now in Gaul, now in Italy, while the Angles, Saxons, and Jutes made a savage reputation in Britain. One historian has written of the invasions from the fourth to the sixth century "Humanity has rarely experienced misery as great as that of this period," and further: "There was no discipline, no moral code to restrain these invaders, who merely added the vices of civilization to the depravity of barbarism. Far from regenerating the world, they very nearly wiped out civilization for ever."[47]

The needless destruction, the savagery, the violence and bloodshed, the deadening effect upon established order in law, economy, and governmental administration, cannot be denied. For many Romans what immediately followed the invasions was worse than what went before. And yet we have learned from Orosius and Salvian that some Romans preferred barbarian to Roman rule, even in the period when Gaulish towns were being burned and villas plundered. We have noted Salvian's strictures upon Roman corruption, viciousness, and brutality, and we have seen that Rome apparently had no aims or rallying points. In short, we have seen every indication that classical civilization in the West had shot its bolt. We have seen above all that the defenders of a superior culture were overwhelmed by a relatively small number of culturally inferior invaders.

The assumption is not paradoxical. Rome only reaped what Rome had sown, and one cannot be sure that, if the tottering structure had not fallen before the frail assaults of barbarian tribesmen, it would not have toppled of its own weight. To what end should the Western Roman world have been "regenerated"? so that civilization could run the same circuit again, all the glories and grandeurs but also the old games and circuses, the heartless oppression, the dullness and pomposity, the stifling of originality and invention, the arrogance, the iniquities of the fiscal system, the *Pax Romana* bought with violence and maintained by despotism?[48] Admittedly the Roman breakdown and the barbarian invasions led to barbarism and superstition; the successors of Rome in the West started with almost nothing and had much to learn. The test of their merit as creators of a civilization was whether they *could* learn, and learn better than their predecessors had learned. It is because they proved to possess this capacity to learn, and ultimately, after long and difficult centuries, to create a civilization which was richer than the Roman, more humane, more conducive to individual dignity and responsibility, that one cannot accept the end of classical civilization in the West as an unmitigated catastrophe.

We have seen evidence of the youthful energy and creative genius of the rising medieval civilization in several fields of human thought and action, in the tremendous inspiration imparted by the new religion through its various agencies, in controversial theology, in vigorous artistic expression and in a new kind of learning and literature, in the indomitable efforts of the missionary monks to convert and civilize the West. We have seen that though commerce suffered grievously, it never wholly stopped, that it shifted its areas of operation and its methods and eventually grew into something stronger than antiquity had ever known. We have seen that in social life men worked out arrangements that were not perfect, but were eminently practical, flexible, capable of improvement as conditions permitted. Even in the sixth and seventh centuries, there is little reason to suppose that common men in Gaul, Spain, Britain, or even Italy were very much worse off than they had been in Rome from Tiberius Gracchus to Diocletian,[49] and the trend was, in the long run, inexorably upward. The foundations laid in the seigniorial and feudal systems have proved stronger than those laid in the Roman Republic. They are admirable not so much in themselves as for what they made possible.

A Changing Society: Technology, Adaptation, and Invention

Until thirty years ago historians paid little attention to technology in the Middle Ages; the general assumption was that, here as elsewhere, stagnation, unrelieved blight, and superstition prevailed. The man responsible above all others for rendering this hoary assumption disreputable was Commandant Lefebvre des Noëttes (d. 1936), a onetime French cavalry officer, who upon his retirement from military life turned his professional training to account by making a historical study of animal power. This work eventually led him to accumulate an impressive body of evidence on technical developments and their social consequences, and to suggest some extremely significant and far-reaching revisions in historical interpretation.[50] Historians have quite properly questioned certain of Lefebvre des Noëttes' conclusions and have subjected his work as a whole to exacting review, but it remains without question one of the capital historical discoveries of recent decades.[51]

We have seen that in Western social life there was a revival, or better a reawakening, of forces which had long lain dormant. Forces long held in subjection were set free to follow their natural course of growth. Something very similar happened in artistic expression. In Gaul, ancient Celtic influences, suppressed during the Roman occupation, contributed to the formation of early medieval and Romanesque art.[52] With the Germanic barbarian invaders, the release was indirect, not a revival but a propagation; they brought to Western Europe designs and forms in jewelry and in such useful ornaments as pins, brooches, and buckles, which they had acquired from Iran and Asia Minor during their sojourn on the coast of the Black Sea.[53] Other innovations were freely borrowed from the Orient—for example, the cupola and the vault, derived from Sassanian Persia, adapted for church construction in Asia Minor, and there observed by Christian pilgrims, who carried the idea home with them.[54]

In many respects early medieval culture seemed to thrive on adversity.[55] In the new economic conditions that grew up after the invasions, for example, there was considerably less need for motive power: "So the decline of the Empire was a good thing for the slave."[56] Violence and upheaval are rarely good in themselves, but they often lead to useful results.[57] Adversity was a very important concomitant of the technological revolution, if that is not too strong a term, which began in the early medieval period.

As noted, influences sometimes came from very distant places and times, e.g., the ancient Celtic and the ancient Oriental,[58] as well as from the classical Mediterranean civilizations. There were also Byzantine, Moslem, and Far Eastern influences, although these were more important in the later than in the earlier medieval period. The exchange was not all one way; there is evidence that Europe gave as well as received, though we do not as yet know much about what came whence and when.[59]

Perhaps the most notable of the early barbarian innovations were in apparel, e.g., trousers and furs; in domestic architecture; in such household appurtenances as felt, skis, butter, barrels, and tubs; and in the cultivation of several new varieties of grain.[60] One wonders why some of these elementary products and processes did not appear, or come into wide usage, sooner—surely some were known before the beginning of the Middle Ages. Was not the reason that new and different social conditions had first to come into existence?[61] Or can everything be explained in terms of geographical conditions, of expanded needs and possibilities, of the steady, unbroken, uninfluenced improvement of techniques?[62] This basic question will be examined a little later.

Meanwhile we may consider briefly some of the most important of the inventions, both native and imported, that began to exert their influence upon the newly forming civilization of the West. Naturally a great many of these are closely connected with agriculture. Those in which Lefebvre des Noëttes first interested himself have to do principally with the horse. He was convinced by his study of documents and of artistic and archaeological evidence that antiquity, in its attempts to use animal motive power, had barely scratched the surface, that its methods of using draft animals were extremely inefficient. One of the chief difficulties derived from the ancient method of harnessing. Horses were harnessed by means of a yoke resting on the withers; oxen by the same method, or by a yoke tied to the horns. The trouble, especially for the horse, was that a strap attached to the yoke above the withers passed around the beast's neck. When he leaned forward to pull, this strap cut into his windpipe and greatly hampered his breathing.⁶³ This drawback—a drawback in every sense, to judge from pictorial and sculptured representations of horses jerking their necks upward and back in order to avoid strangulation—was removed at the beginning of the tenth century or earlier with the introduction of the rigid horse collar resting on the shoulders. Thereafter the horse could lean his full weight into his collar without having his wind cut off.⁶⁴

There were other improvements in harness attachments and apparatus, but after the horse collar Lefebvre des Noëttes considered the principal advances to be the horseshoe and tandem harnessing.⁶⁵ In ancient times the feet of beasts of burden simply wore out if they worked on hard and rocky ground or roads, and a minor foot injury might permanently disable an otherwise healthy animal; oxen were even more vulnerable than horses, since their feet were more tender. The introduction of iron shoes attached by nails made both horses and oxen much more useful and durable servants.⁶⁶ It was customary in antiquity to attach two horses abreast under a yoke—one half-choked horse alone would have been incapable of hauling a load of any size.⁶⁷ Occasionally other horses were put abreast of the first team and connected with them simply by a tether, actually doing none of the work but serving chiefly as replacements. Consequently the system of harnessing in file, or tandem, meant an increase in power limited only by such considerations as maneuverability, space, and terrain.⁶⁸

Lefebvre des Noëttes apparently believed that these new devices were invented in Europe.⁶⁹ Others disagree. Haudricourt, relying largely on etymological evidence, attributes the discovery of the horse collar and shoe to Mongoloid peoples of Asia. He suggests that they were handed on by the Huns to the Germans, Slavs, and Arabs, along with the saddle and stirrup, and were taken West by these peoples. Eastern Europe, according to this view, in having the new kind of harness early, from the fifth to the ninth century, had an advantage over the West.⁷⁰ Roger Grand, a specialist in agricultural history, suggests that the new type of harness was introduced from Scandinavia. His argument runs as follows: The device appeared in Western Europe just after the settling of the Normans in France and the Danish invasions of the British Isles. We know that the Northerners had carts and sleds, and that the Scandinavians were in touch with the Laplanders, who harnessed reindeer to sleds by a breast collar or a light shoulder collar open in front. The Scandinavians and Finns, and possibly also the inhabitants of northern Russia, saw the advantages of this method as opposed to the yoke, which is unsuitable to reindeer because of their bodily structure. Once the idea was recognized, it was a simple matter to apply it also to the harnessing of horses.[71]

None of these three theories may be entirely ruled out, though there are certain conflicts between them: for example, if the Slavs of Eastern Europe had the new harness as early as the fifth century, the Scandinavians could have acquired it from them.[72] As Marc Bloch has commented, nothing is more uncertain than the chronology of this discovery. Our earliest pictorial evidence dates from the tenth century, but medieval artists were notoriously inclined to retain the traditional forms; moreover, they doubtless knew little about the new devices and cared less. Lefebvre des Noëttes himself noted that even after the new harness was established, some artists of the twelfth century represented the horse in the archaic attitude, head pulled back as if to avoid strangulation, though there was no longer any justification for it. Even in the thirteenth century, when the antique harness had virtually disappeared, it was still occasionally pictured in illustrated documents.[73] In all probability the new system was in use in Western Europe well before it was first pictured in a Latin manuscript, probably of French origin, of the early tenth century.[74]

Just how long before the tenth century we cannot say (just as we cannot say much about the *seigneurie* before the ninth century, when "it was unquestionably very old").[75] Unfortunately, more than the satisfaction of idle curiosity depends upon the point. If a technique of such tremendous value and of such revolutionary potentialities was in the hands of Westerners as early as, say, the fifth century, obviously the medieval technological movement was already far advanced. If it was either a barbarian invention or an import, the claim of Roman cultural domination until the eighth century would be still further weakened.

About this last point there can be very little question—the harness was introduced by the barbarians. All the evidence we possess points toward a date several centuries before the first manuscript drawings. Haudricourt, it will be remembered, found philological support for the existence of the new harness in Eastern Europe as early as the fifth century, and he believes that the Ostrogoths took the breast collar to Italy in the same century.[76] If this is true, it may well have moved northward from Italy centuries before the monastic artists took note of it. Very possibly the missionary monks took it with them. There is no evidence to this effect, but the suggestion seems worth making. The improved means of transportation by wagon would have been extremely helpful to the monks in their travels.

Of the other early medieval inventions known to us, one of the more important is the wheeled plow. It seems likely that the Germans either invented this device or brought it to the West, to Gaul and Britain, in very early times. Pliny knew of its existence in Cisalpine Gaul and it may have been known in Britain in Roman times, even though the Romans were not its inventors.[77] Certainly its weight and applicability to heavy soil and to land never before cultivated suggest the Northern plains as its place of origin, just as the lighter *aratrum* came from the Mediterranean lands.[78]

Of the diffusion and use of the heavy wheeled plow in the early Middle Ages, we know nothing. Pictures in manuscripts from England and northern France show nothing but the more familiar *araire* until the later medieval period.[79] Still, it is not hard to make a circumstantial case for its use several centuries earlier. We know that it was useful (specifically, it saved labor and opened up to cultivation rich soils otherwise perforce neglected). We know that the instrument itself existed, and that medieval men were alert enough to see its virtues and proficient enough to put it to use. We know that it could be used in the first place only where community cooperation was already established, as it was on the great estates.[80]

Lynn White, putting aside the disputed question of the date and origin of the heavy plow, links its development and effectiveness with the invention and introduction, attested from the later eighth century, of the three-field system, which measurably increased agricultural production.[81] This method had very great advantages. Not only did it cut down the amount of labor relative to the amount of produce, but it reduced the risks of loss from poor harvests. It was better suited to the more humid and temperate climate of the North, where its labor-saving advantages easily compensated for its disadvantages: more numerous plots and decreased grazing area.[82] In the course of time it made sharper the differentiation between North and South in agricultural methods, use of animals, crops, and living conditions; no factor contributed more to the North's steadily growing prosperity until the time of the great depression of the fourteenth century. Possibly its adoption was stimulated by an increase in population; possibly it was the other way around. In either event, since the three-field system increased food production, it is likely that its spread and the growth of population went hand in hand.[83]

An interesting aspect of the rise of the three-field system is its increasing use of the horse. We know from treatises written late in the Middle Ages that medieval agronomists made serious efforts to weigh accurately the relative efficiency of the two chief draft animals, the ox and the horse. The admirer of the ox counted over his good points thus: The ox is stronger, calmer, and steadier than the horse, and more economical as well, for on soft soils he does not have to be shod, he eats more hay and consequently does not require so much costly oats, and he can be slaughtered for food when old, whereas the horse leaves only his hide. The horse, on the other hand, is defended as much faster than the ox, doing as much work in a day as three or four oxen. To this the champion of the ox could reply that potential speed did not amount to so much, because lazy plowmen would not increase their own speed enough to match it.[84]

Actually the debate was vain; the major regions had already made a choice, and for more practical reasons than calmness and a pleasant disposition. Two factors militated against the horse: some solution to the harnessing problem had to be found before horses could be used profitably for agricultural work, and some way had to be devised to produce large quantities of oats at low cost. The first requirement was met by the horse collar, the second by the three-field system.[85] In the course of time there came to be in medieval Europe a correlation clear enough to discern between the horse and the three-field system and the ox and the two-field system. It appears also, for obvious reasons, that the three-field system was better suited to regions having larger holdings, the two-field system to regions having smaller holdings.[86]

A tremendously important technical apparatus of another kind was the water mill. Although water mills are known to have existed shortly before the birth of Christ, the device was scarcely exploited at all in antiquity.[87] Astonishing though this failure to apply valuable knowledge appears, we know that it was not a rare exception. The ancients, especially from Hellenistic times, discovered many a method or device only to ignore it or merely to play with it: witness Hero's invention of a steam engine. Time after time we see that the responsibility for finding means of putting to work ancient technical ideas and then going on to improvements and fresh discoveries was assumed with alacrity by the successors of the Greeks and Romans, by the Byzantines to some extent but even more by the Moslems and by the medieval Christians of the West.

As Marc Bloch has said, however, an invention is spread abroad only if there is a strong feeling of social necessity, and before the end of the Empire there were such abundant supplies of labor, much of it slave labor, that no such feeling was expressed.[88] Other considerations also enter into the diffusion of inventions, but necessity is essential. The need for the water mill came to be felt toward the end of the Empire, with the decline of slavery.[89] Like other technical improvements of the time, the water mill spread slowly, and older and simpler methods of grinding flour remained in use for centuries.[90] First the monastic authorities, and later secular lords, learned to see substantial advantages for themselves in building water mills to be used by the neighboring peasants, both tenants and others. Beginning with the tenth century, when the great move came to transform established customs into rights, many a lord set up a monopoly for his mill.[91] Here, as in several other instances, the later period developed what the earlier period invented or recognized as opportunity. It is necessary to give credit for the pioneer vision, the ground work, to the early Middle Ages.

Other technical improvements invented or first exploited in the early medieval period might be discussed here, among them the crank, a discovery of fundamental importance in the technological history of Western European civilization and a vast step forward in the acquisition of power devices.[92] Enough has been said, however, to demonstrate the points at issue: the sharp break with the past, the inseparable connection of the new technology with the nature and conditions of the new society in which it grew.

The new methods and devices were so enormously important to the West in the early Middle Ages that it is difficult to know how to begin to weigh them. For one thing, the technological revolution (surely no one will wish to call it a renaissance) brought a vast increase in the amount of productive power at the disposal of Western man, and with it a vast increase in his prospects in fields in which there had previously been no prospects worth the name. The efficient harnessing and shoeing of horses, for example, was significant not only for agriculture, but also for locomotion, hence for communications and transport, hence for construction of all kinds, for conveying food and other produce to towns, for the growth of population, eventually for the expansion of commerce. We might almost speak of an equine revolution. In the new structure of techniques the increase in horse-power was the foundation stone.

It would be difficult to overemphasize the importance of the social consequences of the new power devices. Lefebvre des Noëttes believed that the new inventions destroyed slavery by making it unnecessary and undesirable.[93] Marc Bloch has argued, on the other hand, that the end of slavery came first, creating the necessity to which such devices as the new harness and the water mill were the response. Bloch has very much the better of the argument on narrow grounds, but on wider grounds Lefebvre des Noëttes' claim cannot be altogether dismissed.[94] Bloch rightly stresses the importance throughout the Middle Ages of the Church's opposition to the enslavement of Catholic Christians, but we know that the slave trade continued in spite of this opposition and, in the twelfth and thirteenth centuries, even increased in the South. Granted that slavery never became as important economically as it had been in the Roman Empire, it clearly was far from dead. Indeed it apparently required very little encouragement for new expansion. Was the opposition of the Church the only thing that held it in check? It seems rather that the Church was greatly abetted in this work by the new labor-saving inventions.[95] Lefebvre des Noëttes may have got his chronology confused, but he was eminently correct in his underlying assumption that technological advance entailed a vital blow at slavery and a triumph for freedom.

There is no full and certain explanation of why medieval social necessities brought on a great wave of technical invention and adoption. The Toynbee explanation is unacceptable: such phrases as "the deep sleep of the interregnum (circa A.D. 375–675) which intervened between the break-up of the Roman Empire and the gradual emergence of our Western Society out of the chaos" are the old nonsense, and the view that "our Western Civilization was exposed at its genesis to a challenge from the forests and the rains and the frosts of Transalpine Europe which had not confronted the antecedent Hellenic Civilization" leaves too much out of the reckoning and too many questions unanswered.[96] Were the rains and frosts so very important? Exactly what other causes enter in?

No easy answer will be found, I venture to say, and quite possibly no answer of any kind. Perhaps a serious attempt at explanation would take in so vast a complex of antecedent and contemporary conditions and influences, of native capacities, of unexpected events, disasters, and contributions from other civilizations, as to be unmanageable. For a good many reasons, some of them known and others doubtless unknown, Marc Bloch's social "necessities" came into existence and were recognized by early medieval men, and somehow these necessities were taken care of better, on the technical side, than those of any earlier civilization. But was it only the existence of necessities that brought this about? Do we dare to say that other peoples would have met the same needs, or challenges, as well? What we know is that these founders acted as they did and unchained the greatest technical advance in history. Was this response to a challenge? Perhaps it was, but the roots of the matter lie too deep for Mr. Toynbee's spade.

Lefebvre des Noëttes, after examining the impact of some of the new devices upon slavery, concluded that from the first Capetians down to his own time the West alone benefited from the profound transformation of the means of production and consequently of the social organism, adding that this ten-century head start in technology was in part responsible for the present-day hegemony of the white race.[97] This is a strong statement, but forthright and buttressed by very weighty historical evidence. Many of us today would be inclined, along with Mr. Toynbee, to walk warily indeed in advancing claims of racial superiority or inferiority;[98] perhaps "Western civilization" would be a better term than "white race." No one knows better than the student of ancient and medieval history how much the West owes to other civilizations, above all to the civilizations—and therefore to the races, if you will—of the Orient.

One of the most fertile sources of knowledge from which the new Europe drew, for example, was the great region of steppes in Eastern Europe, Western and Central Asia, and beyond.[99] One striking contribution from this region was the saddle and stirrup. This equipment, together with the development of armor and the breeding of horses large and strong enough to carry an armored rider, greatly altered the relationship between the man on horseback and the man afoot; the ascendancy of horsemen introduced the era of cavalry and eventually the concept of chivalry.[100] The social repercussions of this development are clear: whether or not the military importance of the horse is considered one of the direct causes of feudalism, there can be no doubt that feudalism and cavalry grew up together. By the eighth century or earlier the need for mounted fighting men was apparent, in France at least, and if horses were to be raised, their riders had to be provided with the means, namely landed estates, with which to raise them.[101]

How the equipment which led to the rise of feudal cavalry was introduced into Western Europe is not so easy to trace. Lefebvre des Noëttes was inclined to believe that the Arabs had the stirrup when they invaded Spain. The earliest Latin representations are in Spanish documents of the first half of the ninth century;[102] on the other hand, the very earliest artistic representation of the stirrup known in the West appears to be that of a chess pawn belonging to Charlemagne, traditionally regarded as part of a set of chessmen given to the Frankish ruler by Harun al Rashid.[103] Whatever the date and whatever the details, the origin of the equipment was the East. It was adopted and made a part of the body of Western technical knowledge in very much the way so many other inventions were. Its adoption attests again the flexible and receptive attitude of early medieval men.

It becomes clear, as one examines the problem, that in industrial as well as in other activities the ancient world had lost its capacity to originate. Despite the belated and futile efforts of such emperors as Diocletian and Constantine to increase the use of power machinery,[104] after the first century A.D. simplification and standardization were the order of the day. "No new forms were created, no new ornamental principles introduced. The same sterility reigned in the domain of technique. Save for some new devices in the glass industry, we are unable to detect any new invention in industrial technique after the first century."[105]

How did it happen that after the break-up of the Western Roman Empire, the Occident became so inventive in its own right, so receptive of foreign contributions, so alert to the possibilities of devices that had been available but not availed of for centuries, such as the water mill?[106] That is the basic question.

There is no basic answer. As we have seen in Chapter III, the established patterns of the old civilization had been shaken up and scrambled beyond repair. Later developments demonstrated that whereas many of the pieces would fit well in new patterns, for the most part new pieces were needed. The old buildings had fallen, and could not be rebuilt as they had been. The old architects were dead, and the new architects had new ideas.

In societies and cultures just as in structures of stone and steel the forms, the architecture, the relationships, are paramount. So when the old order collapsed it meant either starting anew or doing without. Whether a new start would be made was up to the successors of Rome in the West. I have contended that the atmosphere in which they reached their decision was fortunate; that the breakdown of age-old set patterns, the formation of a new society, and the recognition of new needs all coincided with a time of conflict, the movement of peoples, adjustment and readjustment, and rapid change. Peoples, customs, and values met and clashed for centuries in the frontier-like society of Western Europe. The exchange of ideas in such an atmosphere was easy. The old restraints upon the introduction, examination, and application of new methods were broken down. In a society in which the supply of manpower was small, a premium was put upon the invention of labor-saving devices. The climate was favorable to exploration and invention, and the soil, so to speak, proved to be rich and productive. There is good reason to believe that if these conditions had not come into existence, all of them together, the great technical advance, which is so fundamental a part of the Western European achievement, could not have been set in motion in the early Middle Ages.

Yet, what has just been said about the impressive early medieval beginning in techniques must also be said about the rest of the four "changes" discussed in this chapter. Not only in technology but in all of them conditions were such as to permit, and even to encourage, an active, positive attitude toward life. It follows at once that the changes made in these various milieux—and they were much more often than not changes for the better—themselves became part of an environment affecting and affected by each of the others, an environment constantly changing through their reciprocal influences upon each other.

The element of freedom stands out, or more accurately, the *preparation* for eventual freedom and individualism and dignity. The deeds and events of the period served a pathfinding function. This was a time when those aforementioned important changes of direction were made, when new goals were headed for. One of those goals, perhaps the most important of all, was freedom—for we can now see and recognize what our predecessors could not discern. Certain fundamental adjustments had to be made before truly significant advances could be made in technology; the West had first to be free from the domination of rigid social institutions obstructive of new methods, free to invent, experiment, borrow, and apply. We have seen how those alterations began to come about in the intellectual sphere, in the changed relation between State and individual, in the honorable position accorded labor through the powerful monastic institution and the missionary activity of the monks, in the status of women through the teachings of Christianity. There was in simple truth a renovation literally from the ground up in the rural, agrarian society of medieval Europe. True, the rights of women, serfs, slaves, individuals in general, long remained theoretical rather than actual, just as, for example, in the feudal system the rights of the king long existed more in theory than in fact.

Theories about rights, freedom, and dignity are dangerous, however— dangerous to tyrannies of all kinds, of ignorance, superstition, poverty, and the rest. A time was to come when kings, in England, in France, in Spain, would turn in their theoretical drafts for the hard cash of political authority. Much later other drafts of theory were to be redeemed in golden realities. From the monks and scholastic philosophers, so long despised as dolts, denied the favor of detached, "scientific" examination, and hence unappreciated, were to come theories and applications which in time would enable Western man further to emancipate himself by winning domination over his physical environment. One of the first of many steps toward freedom from drudgery, for example, came with the development of the horse-drawn heavy plow; the full contributory effect of the scholastic revolution that began with the early theological controversies of the Patristic Age and continued throughout the Middle Ages is only in the process of being investigated.[107] No part of our past has greater power to make intelligible to us how we came to be on the road we now travel. None can make clearer to us the age-old sources of our inspiration and accomplishment.

FIVE

Epilogue on the Past and the Present

Historical study involves a double operation; it both raises questions and seeks answers. It is successful, and hence useful to us, to the extent that it inquires intelligently, imaginatively, and with perspicacity, and obtains its answers by a systematic method, careful probing, and an attitude sufficiently free from blinding prejudices and deadening clichés of thought. If these conditions are not met, we merely exchange old ignorance for new.

On the other hand, not all questions raised by historians can be answered immediately, and some will never be fully answered. Questions of this sort are nonetheless legitimate, and may be useful. The views and interpretations presented in these pages raise a number of such questions. Some of them will be considered in this postscript. No more than general observations, inconclusive and even speculative, may be expected, however—not answers. The response they evoke will be the measure of their value.

The basic contention of this book is that a decisive turning point in the development of the Western tradition was reached in the period between A.D. 300 and 600, when the old pagan classical civilization reached a dead end in the West. What happened in this period had the most far-reaching consequences for later ages. Western civilization might have stopped in its tracks or it might have found no one knows how many ways out of its moribund state. What men of that time actually did, beginning in some fields of human activity even before 300 and continuing on throughout the Carolingian period to about 1000, was to strike out in a new direction in search of new solutions to problems found unsolvable in the Greco-Roman West of ancient times. The uniqueness of the conditions in which the new drive originated is the key to whatever understanding we may hope to acquire of the most recent, longest-range, and most advanced attempt at civilization humanity has made. It has already been remarked that the uniqueness of this attempt lay not only in the peculiar circumstances themselves but also in the combinations of circumstances. Together these led, or enabled, the Europeans of that time to head off, at a sharp angle, in a new direction; where all might have remained at a standstill, a new opportunity was afforded.

It is essential, if we are to grasp the nature of this historical development, that we see it as the discovery of a new, more traversable route through the maze of history. Early medieval men learned, as they were able, both from the past and from the present, as they went along, creating new standards of values and setting up new goals. Just how conscious they were of abandoning old standards and setting new sights, it would be difficult to say. As we have seen, they were not infrequently forced, in spite of themselves, to adopt new methods and values which later turned out to be better than the old.

One of the signal failures of the Roman West had been in the sphere of economics. Although golden opportunities offered themselves, the Romans were unable to establish and maintain a broadly based, balanced economy of enterprise and growth in agriculture and industry with which to feed a healthy and reciprocally invigorating commerce. No doubt their many conquests, their acquisition of great numbers of slaves, their easy extraction of tribute amounting almost to piratical loot, and their contempt for productive labor, ranging from what we should call the highest professions down through business to the poorest agricultural and industrial employment, had much to do with their failure.

Another failure, the fatal maladjustment of society, also defied detection by Romans of the Late Empire. Moralists, in looking back with longing to earlier and happier days, did not discern the real causes of the social troubles of their own times, the political and economic inequalities of opportunity and of justice, the infectious degradation inherent in the institution of slavery, the enormous waste entailed by relegating women to a relatively low and ineffective position in society. They yearned for an ancient time of small independent yeomen, of black bread, earthen pottery, and plain customs. In so doing, they confused simplicity with strength, as if one could not exist without the other.

A third basic failure of the ancient Roman West was in religion. The State religion suffered from the dispiriting exploitation experienced by any religion made an instrument of political convenience. It was in addition cold and austere, quite unembellished by the imagination and vivacity which gave a certain charm to the classical Greek religion before the city-states lost their political freedom and their confident outlook. The State religion was weak in that it condoned or tacitly accepted rigid class distinctions, allowing a privileged position to the aristocracy of wealth and military or official power and assigning a degraded one to the slaves and the poor. The mystery cults which began to gain converts after the conquest of the Eastern Mediterranean did little, if indeed any, better.

These religions seemed incapable of achieving a high moral and ethical standard and, while retaining it, making a universal appeal to all classes and all types. Here lay one of the greatest faults of the ancient pagan religions, namely, in their inability to appreciate the equality of all men in belonging to the human race and possessing a stake in what we now call human dignity. Thence came the special privileges for the powerful and the complacent acceptance of slavery and injustice—and thence, it was to appear later, the fatal weakness. The bond between religion and the State was, in a society inured to privilege on the one hand and exploitation on the other, quite natural, as well as quite ruinous.

Again Romans of the Late Empire could not be expected to see and interpret these weaknesses, not even a sincere devotee of Isis, such as Apuleius in the second, or the pagan philosopher-emperor Julian, who never was able to understand Christianity, in the fourth. St. Augustine broke the tie between the Christian religion and the State, a boon of incalculable value; but even here, as I have already suggested, one may wonder if he could have been aware of all the consequences of such a severance. It scarcely seems possible, and it must also be granted that some Christians, not only in the East but in the West, and not only in remote times but also more recently, have never understood all that the doctrine of the separation of the heavenly and earthly cities involves. Yet in religion, as in economic and social life, whether St. Augustine suspected it or not, the abandonment of the old way and the beginning of a new one denoted a crucial change. This was of course true in the broadest sense, though in this particular discussion I have stressed Christianity's break with an essential characteristic of the old Roman religion, namely, the union of Church and State.

To come back now to the view first mentioned, that the early Middle Ages were unique in affording opportunities for change and that these opportunities were taken advantage of, the old familiar questions of what and why and how arise.

As for the "what," we have seen that a grave collapse of Roman power and order occurred in the West, indicated most clearly by a political, military, and moral breakdown which was inseparably connected with an underlying economic and social failure. Actually to try to distinguish the various aspects of the Western failure from each other is futile; it amounts simply to applying labels to different sides of the same object. The essential fact is that the Roman West, by the time of Constantine or thereabouts, had nowhere to go. The Roman East was able to continue, as we have seen, because it had a stronger economy and a lower standard of living for the masses and also because it was able to stand off or turn aside the barbarian invaders. In this marvelously preserved East there was relatively little change in the centuries following the first barbarian invasions of the West, and what change there was came gradually indeed as compared with the West. For it was in the Occident that the greatest turmoil and upheaval took place, and not just in the third, fourth, and fifth centuries but over and over again for centuries afterward, as wave after wave of invasion swept into Europe. The Western Church, as early as the fifth century or even the fourth, had begun to be at odds with the Eastern, to reveal its increasingly different nature through its diplomacy, its monasticism, and its doctrinal disputes, and also to assume a very different position in the development of civilization.[1]

It is harder to tell all that happened in the West than to tell what it meant. The unprejudiced inquirer, with no racial or national axe to grind—as between Celt and German, Mongol or Slav—is forced to make a roundabout approach to the problem. Perhaps a chemist would be in this position if he had to try to explain why a substance had exploded, without knowing or being able to test directly the chemicals involved.

In the present case we know that an explosion took place, we know the names of at least some of the chemicals, and we have a pretty good idea of the effect wrought by the blast. The roundabout approach here required lies in the necessity for starting sometimes not with the beginning of the action but with its end or effect. Specifically, we have to work back from the change that occurred in Western European civilization to a consideration of the probable and possible causes in human thoughts and deeds. Thus we can tell that changes occurred in the post-Roman period and what they involved, but it is much more difficult to explain exactly what combinations of conditions led to what results and to what kind of results in this period of invasions and so many social and cultural changes. As an example, witness the weary historical cliché that the phenomenon of the collapse of established institutions and the accompanying barbarian invasions, as in the Roman West, was bad, and that the preservation of established institutions and the avoidance of invasion, as in the Roman East, was good.

The assumption seems always to be, somewhat uncritically, that the preservation of any kind of order is good and the disruption of any established institutions at all is deplorable. Good for whom one can only wonder. The failure of Roman power in the West meant, among other things, the decline of slavery, which survived in the more civilized East, as it still does. Also the politically divided and enfeebled West saw the emergence of a Christian Church relatively free to act, specifically to put into effect at least some of its principles, whereas the established East made of its nominally Christian Church a branch of the imperial government. Nor can it be forgotten that the agrarian West, thrown upon its own resources, undergoing repeated incursions of new peoples, but possessing something to swear by and to provide inspiration, set to work, with its hands as well as its brains, and probably as early as the tenth century achieved a standard of living for the bulk of its people superior to that of the urban Roman masses of the golden Age of the Antonines.

For whom was the Roman failure bad? Certainly not for the present age, whose medieval predecessors did so much better a job of discovering and disseminating social advances than the Romans. It needs no saying that the removal of social problems which had been a fundamental obstacle in the way of the ancients left the way open for far-reaching developments in the intellectual and aesthetic realm. The early medieval way of tackling science, that is, by first getting down to earth and working out practical devices, and only then going on to theory, turned out to be vastly superior to the too speculative Greek approach, by air, which never quite got around to coping with crude necessities.

One always returns to the new social milieu of the West, however, when one attempts to get at the essence of what happened. For example, to find out what differentiated the new medieval West from the Byzantine East and the swiftly rising Moslem world, it is necessary in the long run to give thought to basic living conditions. The Byzantine world was, so to speak, born old, for it was the relict of Rome, surviving in its corner of the Mediterranean after the Empire was broken up and stripped of much of its pomp and wealth. It was sedate and settled or, better, set in its ways, worldly-wise, cautious; it knew remarkably well, for the most part, how to conserve and get the most out of its resources. It was urban and civilized, and it possessed a form of Christianity. Its endurance through bad times and good, its shrewd matching of foe against foe, its toughness, its prudence, its glitter, contribute an amazing chapter to history. Eventually, when the adolescent West was grown up enough to understand, Byzantium imparted much. Stable it certainly was, compared with the West, but somewhat in the way Sparta was stable as compared with Athens. Socially it reached a fairly high plateau but there it remained, stratified, conservative, regimented, for centuries. It looked preferably to the past rather than to the future, and made innovations reluctantly when it made them at all.

The Moslem society created by the Arabs was not born old in the Byzantine fashion but it grew up almost overnight. For the Arabs took over, in many areas, a rich, flourishing, urban culture and enlivened it with new leadership and the drive of a new, immediately successful religion. The contrast between the Moslem and the medieval Western world may well be brought out by noting how differently the two acquired classical learning. The Arabs, once they had extended their conquests and entrenched themselves in a position of command, were ready for Greek knowledge; and all this happened in a very short time. It was far different in the West, which had to do its chores, learn to harness horses, plow the soil, and operate mills efficiently before it could take time to read the Greek poets, philosophers, and scientists. The Moslem world, from Baghdad and Damascus across Africa to Spanish Cordova, in our medieval period, was in many respects urbane, refined, learned, rich, and luxurious. It borrowed from the past with speed and applied and extended its learning with brilliance. Its social and economic foundation, however, and its political, or ecclesiastical-political, system may have left something to be desired.

It is strange how little historians have commented on the fact that both the Byzantine and the Moslem civilizations owed as much to the Greeks as did the medieval and modern West.[2] Much has been made, since the Italian Renaissance, of the Western debt to classical antiquity and especially to Greek culture; yet, as mentioned before, the borrower and the conditions of the borrowing are important, as well as what is borrowed. This qualification has rarely been advanced in historical analyses of the origins and growth of the Occident, however, and the erroneous implication, namely, that the Greeks and Romans virtually shaped the West, has gone almost unchallenged. A remarkable inheritance from the Hellenic past, though it might affect the character of Byzantine or Moslem civilization in many ways, could not alter the social foundations on which those civilizations were built. The classical heritage could not rescue the Moslems and Byzantines from fatal social flaws any more than it could save the Romans or the Greeks themselves. It was potentially a powerful cultural force but it did not operate in a social vacuum, either in the East or in the West, in antiquity or in the Middle Ages.

Magnificent though the legacy of Greece and Rome was, it could exert little influence on men who did not understand it, and that was the situation of the agrarian population of the more vigorous portions of the West after the Roman failure. Whereas both Byzantines and Arabs built on long-established social foundations, in character far more Hellenistic than Hellenic, the West had to build anew. In the Eastern societies even the geographical areas, the cities, the trade routes, were in large part old and long familiar. In the West the more important events, developments, and movements were in and toward, first, the little known, uncivilized West and the less known North and, later, the even more barbaric North and East. It was no wonder that the new society grew very slowly as compared with the Moslem world, and that it was both allowed and forced to explore and experiment in ways unheard of among the Byzantines.

The question will naturally arise, whether this slowness on the one hand and speed on the other had any social meaning. Here, with respect to the Eastern civilizations, two factors must again be considered. The first is that in the East the later civilizations, such as the Byzantine and Moslem, though introducing certain new cultural elements in the way of skills, outlooks, and values, built on old social foundations. The ancient, long-established tradition proved too strong there for the religion of Mohammed just as it had for that of Christ. Second, though this applies only to the Moslem civilization, the very speed of the military and political expansion became an adverse factor socially by making almost impossible any fundamental changes in the conquered societies. The old institutions had, too often, to be used, and in being used, they affected the new, sometimes very deeply. In the West, however, the fact that growth was not rapid and easy, not simply a matter of taking over a relatively smooth-running urban culture, may help explain certain very different results. In Western Europe the rise was from a plane equally low in almost all respects, thanks to the leveling effect of the sweeping social, economic, and political changes in the Late Empire and the repeated shock of successive waves of invasion. This no doubt contributed to disrupting old social assumptions concerning the value of such things as labor, the individual, and the state. In a land-based society, forced to cooperate in almost all phases of existence, to work together, to live together in small villages and later towns, where the influence of custom became great but not so great as to preclude change, it was possible for the notion of social partnership, even though more often than not unexpressed, to become a powerful force.[3]

The fact that in the formation of a new society in the West several conditions and forces *occurred together* and reciprocally influenced each other cannot be overemphasized. Is the way to an answer to be found here? Among such forces were (a) Christianity as it came to be in Western conditions, an active and positive moral force and at the same time a cooperative, moving social influence, (b) the violently and abruptly changing social, political, and economic conditions of the Late Empire, (c) the invasions in wave upon wave and in century after century, bringing in new peoples with their new customs, new values, new vigor, and other attributes of a goading and disturbing character, (d) the land-based society and its institutions, differing from earlier agrarian societies because of the nature of its beginnings, a rough-hewn, painfully built society but flexible and tough, and (e) the new technological inventions and adaptations.

In the language of the more recent historians this social revolution and beginning would be described, and quite rightly so, as a "cataclysmic" break with the past.[4] The element of cataclysm itself became a force in the formation of the new society in a time of painfully swift transitions. It became a force because it was by virtue of the thorough shaking-up which the old Roman world of the West experienced that Western Europe was freed of the entrenched but manifestly unadjustable ancient social order. By virtue of later invasions, which were disasters at the time when they occurred, it was able to retain that freedom and encouraged to make the experiments described above.

It will be clear, however, that to attempt to point to just one or two developments clarifies nothing. It was a whole complex of conditions which gave the new society its start. In commenting on the progress of technology in the early Middle Ages, Marc Bloch, one remembers, in a striking phrase referred to a remarkable suppleness and facility of hand, eye, and mind.[5] In speaking of the emergence of the medieval society one may also refer to a remarkable, and fortunate, combination of conditions, events, and talents. At first sight, as I have been at some pains to explain, these new circumstances did not appear likely to lead to much improvement, either in combination or separately, being but a potpourri of old ways and new. Yet in this new world there were, in sufficient quantities, the social necessities that Marc Bloch described as prerequisites to the spreading abroad and application of inventions.[6]

It is a matter of more than passing importance to us to inquire why Christianity became so much more dynamic a social force in the West than in the East. Surely, at least from outward appearances, a great new religion should have been able to do much more in the surviving portion of classical antiquity.[7] Much the same supposition has been made about the Moslem civilization, once so learned, so culturally vigorous, so prosperous. Why did it reach the end of its creative span so quickly? Then there is the question of freedom, which emerged slowly and tortuously out of the wreckage from which the medieval world grew. It seems impossible that it could have come up from such unfavorable conditions, from military defeat and political division, from economic decline and a movement away from towns to the land, from a cultural descent from the Acropolis of Athens to the wranglings of Church Fathers at Ephesus and Chalcedon and the copying of monks in their lonely *scriptoria*.

Eighty years ago Lord Acton, though he did not see all that is now visible, saw more clearly than has anyone else the vital connection between the Middle Ages and the first growth of a kind of liberty broader and more durable than any known to slave-ridden, imperialistic Athens or Rome.[8] Acton recognized that neither the opposition of Christian leaders to slavery alone, nor the Church as an institution alone, nor the Germans alone, nor the townsmen alone, were responsible for resisting and finally breaking through the constant menace of one kind of despotism or another. Rather it was these forces working at the same time, with and upon each other, as in the clash of the feudal hierarchy with the ecclesiastical hierarchy. Although he did not discern the full significance of St. Augustine's careful separation of Christianity from the Empire of his time, he saw in Christ's words, "Render unto Caesar the things that are Caesar's, and unto God the things that are God's" "the repudiation of absolutism and the inauguration of freedom."[9]

Acton was aware also that the ideas of Christianity, which had been introduced in the East as well as in the West, were by themselves not enough; the ideas had to be not merely introduced but applied. The opportunity for their application arose out of the collision of the feudal State and the medieval Church. From that struggle for absolute power came liberty in the form of town franchises, the Estates-General of France, and the Parliament of England. The historian of freedom realized also that the struggle was far from ended with the achievement of certain civil and political rights, and he believed that what began as an intellectual creation of the Athenians and took on flesh and spirit in the Middle Ages still had far to go. Nevertheless, "if there is reason for pride in the past, there is more for hope in the time to come," he said with reference to his native England in 1877.[10] Men of our own time, who must think in terms of a wider need for freedom, might be inclined to grant only that the crisis of liberty is perpetual.

Even Acton, however, with his rare gift of insight, could not detect the wonders of early medieval technological invention and adaptation which Lefebvre des Noëttes was first to discover. It followed that he could not suspect the strength and solidity upon which the agricultural society of medieval Europe was based. Accordingly, while properly depicting the horrors of medieval oppression and violence, he perhaps had a tendency to underestimate the strength of peasant independence and resistance. It was not only by savage and bloody rebellions that the peasantry made known their objections; it was also through constant appeals to custom, through sullen and grudging performance of special work, through flight to other lords, to colonizing expeditions heading East, and eventually to towns. It was partly because medieval peasants were so different from the peasants of antiquity that the medieval towns they created were, among other things, shrewd, tough, and aggressive in extending their liberties.

It would be a mistake, therefore, in attempting to assess the quality of medieval society, to leave out of the reckoning the hard realities of peasant life, the record of slow improvement in circumstances which encouraged the growth of a tradition of stubborn resistance to oppression and of equally stubborn insistence upon certain rights, or customs. This alone was not enough, however, just as Christianity by itself was not enough. It was the alliance of material and spiritual forces that enabled Western society to work out problems which proved too much for excessively practical peoples, such as the ancient Egyptians, or for excessively speculative peoples, such as the Greeks—the fact that the West's spiritual values have been incorporated in its material achievements and have remained almost always inseparable from them.

Perhaps the most valuable thing the West and the world can learn from the past is not to worship it just because it is the past and not to be dominated by it. The meaning lies not in the details in themselves, in the colonate, the Vandal pirate fleet, the conversion of the pagans, the *seigneurie*, or the invention of the stirrup and saddle. These might have varied infinitely. The meaning of the Middle Ages for us lies rather in the general principles, the perception that what mattered historically was the creation of relatively flexible conditions, which did not ruinously hamper experiment but encouraged it and allowed desirable changes to be carried through. Out of these circumstances arose a kind of hardheaded openmindedness toward adaptation to changing conditions rarely to be found in history, and never elsewhere to be found over so long a period.

The large question, which has loomed behind all the rest in the analysis attempted here, is this: If in the early Middle Ages men began to find the way toward liberty, dignity, and decency by striking off the shackles of ignorance, fear, poverty, disease, and despotism, how did they do it? No revolution in human nature took place in that distant time, nor has one yet occurred. The lowest human instincts toward cruelty and oppression, based in selfish greed, in timid, degrading conformity, and in all man's other self-destroying tendencies, flourished hideously in the Middle Ages, as they had before and still do now throughout much of the world. The essential change was not in man. Nor did it come forth magically from Christianity. The influence of the Christian religion was potential. In it existed a generous and challenging doctrine, but man had himself to take the initiative, or rather he had to be free to take it. Nor again was the great change the gift of a classical antiquity which had failed to free itself with all its learning, or of the "Teutonic genius," which has shown itself as prone as any other to victimization by superstition and fantasy. No, the change came because the established forces of conformity were broken and then repeatedly broken again, and because meanwhile men were enabled to apply in practice and to learn by experience from the basic Christian principles. Often, it cannot be denied, the men of early medieval Europe were fortunate. Often it looks to the student of medieval times, as he follows the course of a painful development, as if the game must be up—as if feudal tyranny and oppression, aided by priestly greed and cunning, by peasant ignorance and cruelty, were about to triumph. Time and again the shock of new change came to the rescue. Change was itself the creator of change and of renewed opportunity for change. Constant change proved to be the enemy of closed-mindedness and the unwitting friend of liberty.

Our early medieval predecessors began to win their way, and ours, to freedom because conditions enabled them to learn from the past without being enslaved by it. What they learned with difficulty we may learn at much less cost. It is to keep conditions, including preeminently the attitude of the mind, open to change; to greet change, when it comes, with intelligent curiosity; to examine it with care; to apply the tests of human dignity and freedom to it; and above all, to avoid the easy, thoughtless, stifling, almost automatic negative dictated without reason by fear, laziness, and smug self-satisfaction.

As R. G. Collingwood has pointed out, progress is not merely something to be discovered by historical thought; "it is only through historical thinking that it comes about at all."[11] There was a time when the worst enemy of the new West, struggling to build civilization in the early Middle Ages, was the old West. Medieval men, happily for them and for us, found a way to keep much of the best of the classical past while discarding the worst of it. It should not be insurmountably difficult for a historically alert modern world to maintain the tradition.

Notes

1. Michael Rostovtzeff, *The Social and Economic History of the Roman Empire* (Oxford, 1926), pp. 486–87.

2. Elmer Davis, "Are We Worth Saving? And If So, Why?" in *But We Were Born Free* (Indianapolis and New York, 1953), p. 217.

3. An extensive literature on the subject has now accumulated. For brief and convenient comments and, in the last two works cited, for useful references, see H. M. Gwatkin and J. P. Whitney, "Preface to Volume I," *The Cambridge Medieval History*, 2d ed. (Cambridge, England, 1924), I, vii–ix, and Gwatkin, 1–2 (the first edition appeared in 1911); Ferdinand Lot, "Introduction," *Histoire du Moyen Age*, I, première partie, *Les Destinées de l'Empire en Occident de 395 à 768* (Paris, 1940), pp. 1–3; and Herman Aubin, "Die Frage nach der Scheide zwischen Altertum und Mittelalter," *Historische Zeitschrift*, CLXXII (October 1951), 245–63. See also the sketch given by Oscar Halecki in "Bulletin du centre international de synthèse, Section de synthèse historique," No. 2 (December 1926), pp. 16–22, appended to *Revue de synthèse historique*, XLII (1926). Many others might be cited, but I shall add only Herbert Butterfield, *Man on His Past. The Study of the History of Historical Scholarship* (Cambridge, England, 1955). His discussion, which comes as a part of a consideration of the problems of universal or general history, is, for that reason, particularly meaningful. See especially pp. 44 ff. Note also Paul Lehmann's recent remarks on terminology, "Das Problem der karolingischen Renaissance," in *Settimane di studio del centro italiano di studi sull'alto medioevo*, I. *I Problemi della civiltà carolingia* (Spoleto, 1954), pp. 309–58, and also the shrewd and amusing analysis of renaissances presented by Angelo Monteverdi, "Il Problema del rinascimento carolino," *ibid.*, pp. 359–72, especially pp. 366–72. Cf. "La Discussione" which follows Monteverdi's paper, pp. 373–77. This collection of learned papers will hereafter be cited as *Settimane di studio*.

4. "The Present Problems of Medieval History," *International Congress of Arts and Science*, edited by Howard J. Rogers, Vol. III (London and New York, 1906), pp. 126–28. The description of Adams as "dean of American medievalists" is that of James Westfall Thompson, "Profitable Fields of Investigation in Medieval History," *American Historical Review*, XVIII (1913), 490. It will be noted that Thompson's dissenting opinion followed only a few years after publication of Adams' pronouncement. Among American medievalists, however, Adams' view long prevailed over Thompson's belief (*loc. cit.*, p. 491) that "Much analytical work may yet frequently be done and with profit in new study of an old subject." For that matter it is surprising, to say no more, that a medievalist may still be found to say that the period was unimportant anyway,

apparently upon the principle that paucity of evidence is a sure indication of paucity of history; e.g., Bryce D. Lyon, in a review of Robert Latouche's valuable study, *Les Origines de l'économie occidentale (IVe–XIe siècle)* (Paris, 1956), declares that "Perhaps, after all, the old-fashioned historians were right when they concluded that the early Middle Ages were relatively dead centuries," *American Historical Review*, LXII (1957), 375.

5. As Herbert Butterfield has remarked in a review of Geoffrey Barraclough, *History in a Changing World* (Oxford, 1955) in *The Cambridge Historical Journal*, XII (1956), 189–91, it is essential for Western man, in attempting to deal with the problems of the present, to know the sources of his culture.

NOTES TO CHAPTER II

The thesis first appeared in written form in an article published in 1922 in the *Revue belge de philologie et d'histoire*. It was taken up subsequently in a number of works and assumed its final form in the book *Mahomet et Charlemagne*, which was finished in 1935, only a short time before Pirenne's death, and was published two years later under the direction of the author's son and one of his former students, Fernand Vercauteren. In the following pages references are to the second French edition, Paris and Brussels, 1937. Gray Cowan Boyce in "The Legacy of Henri Pirenne," *Byzantion*, XV (1940–41), 449–64, has given a brief but eloquent and informative sketch of Pirenne's aims, methods, and accomplishments. Similar testimonials have been written by disciples and colleagues of the Belgian master in other countries. On his earlier and later interest in early medieval history see also F. M. Powicke, *Modern Historians and the Study of History. Essays and Papers* (London, 1955), p. 97. See for a survey chiefly of the economic aspects of the thesis and for bibliographical purposes Anne Riising, "The Fate of Henri Pirenne's Thesis on the Consequences of the Islamic Expansion," *Classica et Medievalia*, XIII (1952), 87–130. I have been unable to consult Robert Lopez's report on East and West in the Early Middle Ages presented at the Tenth International Congress of the Historical Sciences, meeting at Rome in 1955.

2. Pirenne, *Mahomet*, p. 210.

3. *Ibid.,* pp. 40–43.

4. *Ibid.,* pp. 260–61, and note Einar Joranson's discerning review, *American Historical Review*, XLIV (1938–39), 324–25. Note the contrast drawn between the early Germanic invaders, Slavs, Arabs, Normans, and Hungarians, by Fritz Kaphan, *Zwischen Antike und Mittelalter. Das Donau-Alpenland im Zeitalter St. Severins* (Munich, ca. 1946), pp. 204 ff. and 208 ff.

5. Pirenne, *Mahomet*, p. 123. See Eileen Power's review of Bernard Miall's English translation of Pirenne, *Mohammed and Charlemagne* (New York, 1939), in *Economic History Review*, X (1939–40), 60–62; Norman Baynes's review, in *Journal of Roman Studies*, XIX (1929), 224–35, of Pirenne's *Les Villes du moyen âge*, Ferdinand Lot's *La Fin du monde antique et le début du moyen*

âge, and Rostovtzeff's *Social and Economic History of the Roman Empire.* See also André Piganiol, *L'Empire chrétien (325-395)* (Tome IV, Part II, of *Histoire romaine,* ed. Gustave Glotz; Paris, 1947), p. 422, and Ferdinand Lot, *La Fin du monde antique,* rev. ed. (Paris, 1951), p. 531. This work will hereafter be cited as Lot, FMA.

6. Further light on the status of the two parts of the Empire, the *pars occidentis* and the *pars orientis,* is supplied by Émilienne Demougeot, *De l'Unité à la division de l'empire romain, 395-410: Essai sur le gouvernement impérial* (Paris, 1951). See also Robert Latouche, *Les Grandes Invasions et la crise de l'Occident au Ve siècle* (Paris, 1946), pp. 258-59; for Latouche's most recent word on the subject, see *Les Origines de l'économie occidentale* (Paris, 1956), pp. 138 ff.

7. Pirenne, *Mahomet,* pp. 98-99.

8. *Ibid.,* p. 126.

9. See Baynes's review, *loc. cit.,* pp. 224-35. See also his article "The Decline of the Roman Power in Western Europe. Some Modern Explanations," *Journal of Roman Studies,* XXXIII (1943), 29-35. Archibald R. Lewis, *Naval Power and Trade in the Mediterranean, A.D. 500-1100* (Princeton, 1951), p. 19, n. 58, believes that Baynes exaggerates the role of Vandal sea power.

10. François Ganshof, "Note sur les ports de Provence du VIIIe au Xe siècle," *Revue historique,* CLXXXIII (1938), 28-37, and Robert S. Lopez, "Mohammed and Charlemagne: a Revision," *Speculum,* XVIII (1943), 14-38. Note also Lopez's reference to Étienne Sabbe, "L'Importation des tissus orientaux en Europe occidentale au haut moyen âge," *Revue belge de philologie et d'histoire,* XIV (1935), 811-48, 1261-88. Joseph Calmette, *Charlemagne. Sa vie et son oeuvre* (Paris, 1945), pp. 235-36 and p. 249, n. 4, has noted that some of the strongest blows against certain of Pirenne's economic theories have been delivered by his own students. Boyce, *loc. cit.,* p. 459, n. 23, also refers to some of the opposing views expressed by students of Pirenne's.

11. Lopez, "Mohammed and Charlemagne," *loc. cit.,* pp. 19, 35, 37, and Rostovtzeff, "The Decay of the Ancient World and Its Economic Explanations," *Economic History Review,* II (1930), 197-99. Lot, in a posthumously published work, *Nouvelles Recherches sur l'impôt foncier et la capitation personnelle sous le Bas-Empire* (fasc. 304 of Bibliothèque de l'École des Hautes Études; Paris, 1955), p. 179, also makes some interesting comments on this subject.

12. Henri Pirenne, "The Place of the Netherlands in the Economic History of Mediaeval Europe," *Economic History Review,* Vol. II, No. 2 (1929), p. 22. In this article Pirenne also suggests (p. 24), in speaking of the cause of the sudden descent of the Northmen on England and the Continent in the ninth century, that "it is extremely probable that it may be considered from some points of view as a consequence of the invasion of Islam." It is at least equally probable that the movement was as independent of the Saracens as the earlier Germanic or Slavic and Mongoloid incursions and would have taken place even if there had been no Saracenic conquest.

13. See Daniel C. Dennett, Jr., "Pirenne and Muhammad," *Speculum,* XXIII (1948), 178–80, on the nature of Gallic products of an earlier period of prosperity, and on the changes that had taken place by the beginning of the Frankish period. See also the remarkable studies of Maurice Lombard, "Les Bases monétaires d'une suprématie économique. L'or musulman du VIIIe au XIe siècle," *Annales,* Vol. II, No. 2 (1947), pp. 143–60, and "Mahomet et Charlemagne. Le problème économique," *Annales,* Vol. III, No. 2 (1948), pp. 188–99. In the first article (pp. 143–44) Lombard holds that the trade carried on by Levantine merchants with the barbarian West was exclusively a commerce of importation. The Western lands had nothing desired by the East with which to pay for their imports, save gold. When the supply of Western gold became too small, the Levantines lost interest.

14. Dennett, *loc. cit.,* p. 186. Cf. Lewis, *Naval Power,* pp. 12–13, 45–47, and Lot, *Les Destinées de l'Empire en Occident de 395 à 888* (Tome I of the *Histoire du moyen âge* in the *Histoire générale* edited by Gustave Glotz; Paris, 1940), p. 302. For a discussion of the size of Gallic towns in the Later Empire and after, see Lot, FMA, pp. 80–83, 517, and the reference there to his ingenious population study, *Recherches sur la population et la superficie des cités remontant à la période gallo-romaine* (Paris, 1945–47 and 1950).

15. See Dennett's remarks, *loc. cit.,* pp. 186–88.

16. See, for example, Gregory of Tours, *Historia Francorum,* VII, 45–46, where a good deal is made out of almost nothing.

17. Pirenne, *Mahomet,* pp. 40–42.

18. Lot, *Destinées de l'Empire,* pp. 315–16, clearly delineates the greedy, grasping, wasteful, and useless character of these kings. See also his *L'Impôt foncier et la capitation personnelle sous le Bas-Empire et à l'époque franque* (Paris, 1928), pp. 99–100; this work, cited hereafter as *L'Impôt foncier,* should not be confused with the posthumous work referred to in note 11. For that matter, Pirenne, *Mahomet,* pp. 40–42, makes no secret of the Merovingian greed.

19. Cf. G. I. Bratianu, "La Distribution de l'or et les raisons économiques de la division de l'empire romain," in *Études byzantines d'histoire économique et sociale* (Paris, 1938), pp. 57–91; see especially pp. 75–76 and his useful references throughout. Bratianu makes all possible concessions to the Pirenne thesis (see, for example, pp. 75 and 77), but the total effect of his work is extremely damaging to it.

20. See, for example, Lot, *Destinées de l'Empire,* p. 316.

21. See Fustel de Coulanges, *Les Transformations de la royauté pendant l'époque carolingienne* (Paris, 1892), p. 29, and note Pirenne's references to this and subsequent passages of Fustel's, *Mahomet,* pp. 171 f. Pirenne here seems to have fallen into a contradiction, for he says both that the land tax comprised the major part of the Merovingian kings' revenue and that the commercial toll was by far the most important part of their resources. He recognized that they did not know the value of their lands and the income from them, but had difficulty explaining what happened to the land tax as compared with the com-

mercial toll. See Fustel, *Transformations*, pp. 30, 36 ff., 40, and Silvester Hofbauer, *Die Ausbildung der grossen Grandherrschaften im Reiche der Merowinger* (Vienna, 1927), pp. 91 ff., on the growth of the nobility's economic and political power and on the declining land taxes. Gregory of Tours, *Historia Francorum*, V, 28, 34, throws an interesting light on the Church's connection with the monarchy's surrender of the land tax. See also Lot, *Destinées de l'Empire*, pp. 315–16.

22. Cf. Pirenne, *Mahomet*, p. 172; Fustel de Coulanges, *Transformations*, pp. 37–40; Lot, *Destinées de l'Empire*, pp. 316–17, and *L'Impôt foncier*, pp. 103, 106. Note that in *L'Impôt foncier*, p. 106, n. 2, Lot cautions that Fustel, in his extensive examination of immunities in *Les Origines du système féodal. Le bénéfice et le patronat pendant l'époque mérovingienne* (Paris, 1890), used for the Merovingian era diplomas forged or remade in the Carolingian era. Even so the large significance of Fustel's views concerning immunities stands unimpaired. Fustel was aware that all the diplomas were not equally authentic, *Le Bénéfice*, p. 344. Lot, *L'Impôt foncier*, p. 106, agrees that in the course of the sixth and seventh centuries most bishoprics and monasteries were given exemption and that many lay magnates fared as well. He notes also that these laymen acquired exemption not always by royal favor but sometimes by force. Maurice Kroell, *L'Immunité franque* (Paris, 1910), pp. 333–59, lists both the diplomas known to be authentic and those recognized as false.

23. Pirenne, *Mahomet*, pp. 172–73.

24. *Ibid.*, p. 173.

25. Note Lot's summary, *L'Impôt foncier*, pp. 86, 124–25. See also Lot, *Destinées de l'Empire*, pp. 315–16, and Gregory of Tours, V, 28, 34.

26. Rostovtzeff, "The Decay of the Ancient World," *loc. cit.*, pp. 197–99. See also H. St. L. B. Moss, "The Economic Consequences of the Barbarian Invasions," *Economic History Review*, VII (1936–37), 210, 214; offering an analysis of certain economic views of Pirenne and the Austrian master, Alfons Dopsch, Moss appropriately asks what has become of Rostovtzeff's "great change." Moss interprets the "closed house-economy" of Western Europe ca. 800 as "directly due to the breakdown of Roman government, communications, and trade," and places the turning point in the period A.D. 235–85. This half-century has been recognized by many specialists in the earlier period, if not by Pirenne and others who have worked back from a later to an earlier period, as a time of vital, drastic change, perhaps the most decisive of a number of turning points in the period from ca. 180 to ca. 500. Attention should also be called to a little group of articles debating Pirenne's views on the origins of the dominant merchant class in the newly rising towns of the Middle Ages. The debate concerns a later period than the subject of this paper, but certain remarks are pertinent. Lucien Febvre introduces the subject with a sketch entitled "Fils de riches ou nouveaux riches?" *Annales*, Vol I, No. 2 (1946), pp. 139–42. Then comes the article "Les Origines du patriciat urbain. Henri Pirenne s'est-il trompé?" Part I, "La Thèse," pp. 143–48, is by the Abbé Jean Lestocquoy, and

Part II, "La Discussion," pp. 148–53, by Georges Espinas. Febvre points out that Pirenne introduced this thesis at the International Historical Congress at London in 1913, and that his address was published in English the following year in the *American Historical Review*. In the course of the discussion it is mentioned that Pirenne had a tendency to generalize somewhat too easily from localized evidence with which he was thoroughly familiar, and to extend his findings to cover a much larger area. As Febvre put it (p. 139), "Que Pirenne ait mal connu l'Italie, c'est un fait. Il ne le cachait point. Il travaillait sur documents nordiques. . . . Il ne s'est beaucoup enquis ni du Midi, ni de l'Italie." Espinas, in presenting his objections, observes (p. 148), "Il est evident ici, que le grand historien qu'était Henri Pirenne, voyait—et devait voir—les choses de haut. Peut-être, malgré cette sort de divination qu'il semblait posséder, les voyait-il parfois, malgré lui, d'un peu trop haut." See also Lestocquoy, "The Tenth Century," *Economic History Review*, XVII (1947), 1–14.

27. Pirenne, *Mahomet*, pp. 62–78. His evidence is sometimes strange; note *Mahomet*, p. 83, and compare Lot, *Destinées de l'Empire*, pp. 365–66. On the Oriental merchants see Lombard, "L'Or musulman," *loc. cit.*, p. 144; Dennett, "Pirenne," *loc. cit.*, p. 187; and, above all, Édouard Salin, *La Civilisation mérovingienne d'après les sépultures, les textes et le laboratoire* (Première partie, *Les Idées et les faits*; Paris, 1949), pp. 143–51 and 201–4.

28. At the beginning of his discussion of Oriental navigation (*Mahomet*, p. 62), he thought it sufficient to note only that of the two parts of the Empire, the Greek was always more advanced in civilization than the Latin. "Inutile d'insister sur ce fait évident." It was not a matter of insisting on it at all, of course, but of explaining it.

29. See Bratianu, "La Distribution de l'or," *loc. cit.*, and also "Une Nouvelle Histoire de l'Europe au moyen âge: la fin du monde antique et le triomphe de l'orient," *Revue belge de philologie et d'histoire*, XVIII (1939), 252–66. The production of works on coinage and the precious metals in general during the Middle Ages has been large and steady in recent decades, and it appears that the subject will continue to attract attention. The works of Dopsch, Mickwitz, Cipolla, and Marc Bloch are useful for the period under discussion, but almost all of the larger studies by specialists in the period, e.g., Stein, Lot, Rostovtzeff, and Pirenne, have had something pertinent to say. Note also more recently Sture Bolin, "Mohammed, Charlemagne and Ruric," *The Scandinavian Economic History Review*, I (1953), 5–39, and Édouard Perroy, "Encore Mahomet et Charlemagne," *Revue historique*, CCXII (1954), 232–38, and their citations.

30. Note Eileen Power's reference to this point in her review of Pirenne's *Mohammed and Charlemagne, loc. cit.*, p. 61. See also J. Brutzkus, "Trade with Eastern Europe, 800–1200," *Economic History Review*, XIII (1943), 31–41, an article submitted in 1937, translated and rearranged by M. M. Postan and Eileen Power, and published after the author's death. We find here further evidence that trade continued after the Saracenic expansion, but obviously it was not of

sufficient volume to enrich the West. See also Bolin, *loc. cit.*, pp. 24 ff., for some interesting views which the author promises soon to state more fully.

31. See Salin, *La Civilisation mérovingienne*, pp. 202 ff.

32. *Ibid.*, p. 202. See also Lestocquoy, "De l'Unité à la pluralité: le paysage urbain en Gaule du Ve au IXe siècle," *Annales*, VIII (1953), 159–72, on the shrinking of towns.

33. See Lombard, "Mahomet et Charlemagne," *loc. cit.*, pp. 196–99.

34. Lot, *Les Invasions germaniques. La pénétration mutuelle du monde barbare et du monde romain* (Paris, 1945), pp. 151 ff. "Cependant la domination byzantine se serait peut-être prolongée, bien que péniblement, sans l'accident imprévisible de la naissance et de l'expansion de l'Islam." This would have been a respite of dubious value.

35. I refer to the Roman authorities' failure to develop a workable free-enterprise system to supplant the old system of preying in various ways upon the truly productive areas of the Empire, drawing sustenance from them to Rome and Italy and giving in return, at least for a time, unified administration and protection. See Lot's recent comments, *La Gaule. Les fondements ethniques, sociaux et politiques de la nation française* (Paris, 1947), pp. 386–87. Among the developments that led to the birth of a new economy in medieval Europe—for it was quite different from that of antiquity—I should of course include more than the Moslems' wealth and desire to find new markets and new sources of supply. Very important indeed, for example, were technical improvements in agricultural methods (see Calmette, *Le Monde féodal*, pp. 209–10), which made medieval European agriculture in some respects superior to that of the ancient and Byzantine worlds.

36. See the lively and interesting pronouncements of Carlo M. Cipolla, "Encore Mahomet et Charlemagne. L'économie politique au secours de l'histoire. Sur une façon de comprendre l'histoire qui est nôtre," *Annales*, IV (1949), 4–9, with a brief introduction by Lucien Febvre. Cipolla concludes, "Le haut moyen âge, période caractérisée par l'absence de toute forme de division du travail, par un rendement réel minime, par une tendance déflationniste forte et prolongée, par une balance commerciale nettement défavorable à l'Europe, commence approximativement au Ve siècle et finit approximativement au XIe siècle." Cf. the opinion of Lopez, "Du Marché temporaire à la colonie permanente. L'évolution de la politique commerciale au moyen âge," *Annales*, IV (1949), 389–405, who says (p. 390), "Le haut moyen âge commence, à plusieurs égards, au Bas-Empire romain: c'est à dire au moment ou l'horizon du commerce et des marchands, qui n'avait jamais été brillant s'assombrit de plus en plus. Avant le IVe siècle, il y avait déjà un cercle vicieux. . . . Après le IVe siècle, c'est une descente rapide." For an admirable description of the close relationship between political and economic realities in the late imperial epoch, see Lopez's whole discussion of this topic, pp. 390–92. Cf. Lot, *La Gaule*, pp. 380, 384.

37. Pirenne, *Mahomet*, pp. 247–48.

38. We know that many Roman institutions survived in Merovingian Gaul, but there were also important German innovations, such as grants of immunities. Dennett, *loc. cit.*, pp. 184–85, would account for the granting of immunities as early as the sixth century as a "short-sighted act" and a cause of the king's weakness. Pirenne, it will be remembered, regards the immunities not as the cause but rather as a consequence of the king's weakness, originating in his loss of revenue (*Mahomet*, pp. 172–73). As we have seen, however, the disease was much more deep-seated than either explanation would indicate, and arose from the king's long-continued failure to govern. This failure had several causes and was doubtless related to the similar failure of the last of the Western emperors, as suggested above. Certainly in considering this question the recent work of Mlle Demougeot, cited above, should be considered, especially Part III, where she contrasts the general state of the East and West in 410. See also the accounts of Christopher Dawson, *The Making of Europe. An Introduction to the History of European Unity* (London, 1948), pp. 76–77, and Latouche, *Les Grandes Invasions*, pp. 231 ff., 244–47.

39. *Philosophiae Consolatio*, edited by Edward K. Rand and Hugh F. Stewart (New York, 1918), I, iv, 34–51. See also Ernest Stein, *Histoire du Bas-Empire*, Tome II, *De la disparition de l'Empire d'Occident à la mort de Justinien (476–565)* (Paris-Brussels-Amsterdam, 1949), pp. 121–22, 254 ff.

40. Pirenne, *Mahomet*, pp. 142–43.

41. *Ibid.*, p. 142.

42. *Ibid.*, pp. 155–57.

43. Some time after writing these words I noted that Lewis, *Naval Power*, p. 97, says virtually the same thing, i.e., that Pirenne "picked the wrong villain" and that "it was not the Arabs but Byzantium who destroyed the ancient unity of the Mediterranean."

44. On Venice's trade with the Moslems, see Pirenne, *Mahomet*, pp. 157–60.

45. Lewis, *Naval Power*, pp. 95–96.

46. Pirenne, *Mahomet*, pp. 123–24.

47. Cf. Salin, *La Civilisation mérovingienne*, p. 203.

48. As Joranson, *loc. cit.*, pp. 324–25, has noted.

49. Pirenne, *Mahomet*, pp. 252–55.

50. *Ibid.*, p. 102.

51. *Ibid.*, pp. 101–4, 106–7, 110–11.

52. Although it is true, as mentioned above, that Pirenne was unable to make revisions or changes before the publication of the *Mahomet et Charlemagne*, it is quite clear that the basic thesis had long been completely worked out.

53. Pirenne, *Mahomet*, p. 102.

54. Pirenne rightly attributed Boethius's execution to his implication in a conspiracy with the Byzantine court, but was unaware of the theological aspect of the plot (*Mahomet*, p. 103). I refer to this affair in an article published several years after Pirenne's death, "Theodoric vs. Boethius: Vindication and Apology,"

American Historical Review, XLIX (1944), 410–26. The *opuscula sacra* ought to have been mentioned even in a brief sketch of Boethius's intellectual interests in relationship to his age.

55. Pirenne, *Mahomet,* pp. 102–4. But see Pierre de Labriolle, *Histoire de la littérature latine chrétienne,* 3d ed., revised and expanded by Gustave Bardy (Paris, 1947), p. 12, n. 1. Bardy points out in this note that the sterility widespread among pagan rhetoricians from the end of the fourth century is evident among certain Christian writers as well, among whom Ennodius is the most vapid of the vapid.

56. For an incisive and reliable interpretation of the formation of the new tradition in literature see M. L. W. Laistner, *Thought and Letters in Western Europe, A.D. 500–900,* 2d ed. (Ithaca, N.Y., 1957), pp. 49–53, and Dawson, *Making of Europe,* pp. 38–53. Dawson remarks (pp. 52–53), in speaking of Cassiodorus, "As with Gregory Nazianzen and Augustine, the arts are regarded as an instrument of religious education, not as an end in themselves," and "Thus Vivarium was the starting-point of the tradition of monastic learning."

57. *Mahomet,* p. 111; a different view was presented a little before (p. 106), when Pirenne mentioned Gregory's reproach to Desiderius of Vienne and concluded that the old intellectual life continued to the seventh century. Pirenne oversimplified a complex situation. For an understanding of the complexities involved, see Laistner, "Pagan Schools and Christian Teachers," in *Liber Floridus. Mittellateinische Studien,* Festschrift Paul Lehmann, ed. Bernhard Bischoff and Suso Brechter (Erzabtei St. Ottilien, 1950), pp. 47–61. See also the same author's comment in *Christianity and Pagan Culture in the Later Roman Empire together with an English Translation of John Chrysostom's Address on Vainglory and the Right Way for Parents to Bring Up Their Children* (Ithaca, N.Y., 1951), p. 24. I do not quarrel with Pirenne's insistence that Christian teachers used classical works. This fact requires no repetition. Much of the old was absorbed in the formation of a new world, but, as Laistner observes, it was in "a new and wholly Christian world" that the classical tradition lived on.

58. Laistner, *Thought and Letters,* pp. 126–27. See also Lot, FMA, p. 529 f.

59. Pirenne, *Mahomet,* p. 112. It would be equally erroneous to maintain that the appearance of good vernacular writing in the twelfth and thirteenth centuries meant the end of Latin. See Ernst R. Curtius, *Europäische Literatur und lateinisches Mittelalter* (Bern, 1948), pp. 33–34.

60. See Einar Löfstedt, *Coniectanea. Untersuchungen auf dem Gebiete der antiken und mittelalterlichen Latinität* (Uppsala and Stockholm, 1950), pp. 3–4. As a further corrective to Pirenne's narrowness on this subject, see Luitpold Wallach, "Education and Culture in the Tenth Century," *Medievalia et Humanistica,* IX (1955), 18–22.

61. Curtius, *Europäische Literatur,* p. 35.

62. Labriolle, *Littérature latine chrétienne,* pp. 12–13. Despite the faults of the Christian writers, such as their acceptance of the rhetorical tastes of their age, they did not simply play with literature, as did the pagan writers. The Chris-

tians, says Labriolle, "believed in what they said; they spoke from the heart; their whole moral being was involved in their writings."

63. Of the *Rule for Monks* Pirenne remarked that it chiefly owed its future universal importance to the proximity of Rome. Compare with this restrained and rather grudging praise the view of G. G. Coulton, *The Medieval Scene* (New York, 1931), p. 76, who calls it "a model of practical and spiritual wisdom combined" and adds with evident approval that "it has been called the greatest document of the whole Middle Ages." Coulton, of course, is but one of a great many medieval historians thus to eulogize Benedict's *Rule*; but he was not one to praise the work of monks casually.

64. Pirenne, *Mahomet*, p. 111.

65. Henri-Irénée Marrou, *Histoire de l'éducation dans l'antiquité* (Paris, 1948), pp. 569–70.

66. *Ibid.*, pp. 452–61.

67. *Ibid.*, p. 447, but see all of chap. 10, "L'Apparition des écoles chrétiennes de type médiéval," pp. 435–47.

68. Pirenne, *Mahomet*, pp. 120–21. He refers also to an earlier treatment of the subject, "De l'État de l'instruction des laïques à l'époque mérovingienne," *Revue bénédictine*, XLVI (1934), 165, and adds that even among the Lombards such schools survived. Giuseppe Salvioli, *L'Istruzione pubblica in Italia nei secoli VIII, IX, e X* (Florence, 1898), p. 14, also mentions a lay school in Italy in the Lombard period but offers no supporting evidence.

69. Marrou, *Histoire de l'éducation*, pp. 569–70. And note Wallach, *loc. cit.*, p. 20.

70. Pirenne, *Mahomet*, p. 111.

71. *Ibid.*, pp. 112, 118. Cf. the view of Lot, FMA, p. 523, that the art of Europe underwent a complete and rapid transformation after the end of the third century.

72. Lot, FMA, pp. 115, 157, 168–71.

73. See Henri Focillon, *Moyen Âge: Survivances et réveils. Études d'art et d'histoire* (Montreal, 1945), pp. 31–53, particularly pp. 31–42. See also Salin, *La Civilisation mérovingienne*, p. 203, and again Lot's very informative comments and quotations, FMA, pp. 540–43, which help to illustrate the complexity as well as the fascination of this subject. Note especially the references to the recent works, some of which I have not been able to consult, of Émile Mâle, Jean Hubert, and Françoise Henry, the last a disciple of Focillon's. As remarked above, research in this subject has been extensive, and the results have appeared in monographs and journals which are sometimes difficult to obtain in this country.

74. Pirenne, *Mahomet*, pp. 112 ff. See also Focillon's later work, *L'An mil* (Paris, 1952), pp. 14–15.

75. Focillon, *Moyen Âge*, pp. 36–38. See also Focillon, *L'An mil*, pp. 12–15, for the changes introduced by the Germans, including their psychological impact. Note especially the keen observation that the invaders of the Empire really

belonged to the prehistoric period, pp. 13–14. Erna Patzelt, in *Die fränkische Kultur und der Islam mit besonderer Berücksichtigung der nordischen Entwicklung* (Baden, 1932), had also noted this important, and commonly unrecognized, connection. Note the very interesting evidence which she presents in her third chapter, "Die Bedeutung des Nordens für die Entwicklung Europas in frühgermanischer Zeit," pp. 62–157.

76. Focillon, *Moyen Age*, p. 41, and Lot, FMA, pp. 540–43.

77. Pirenne, *Mahomet*, pp. 191–92, 200. Henri Grégoire, "The Byzantine Church," in *Byzantium. An Introduction to East Roman Civilization*, ed. Norman H. Baynes and H. St.L. B. Moss (Oxford, 1948), pp. 120–21, would not agree with the view that the divisions between East and West caused by the Christological disputes were permanent. He adds that the eighth-century popes did not free themselves from the control of the Byzantine emperor until it became clear that he had "neither the strength nor the leisure to defend them against Lombards and Arabs."

78. Joranson, *loc. cit.*, pp. 324–25.

79. Justinian's later efforts were equally unavailing, and the Monophysites of Syria and Egypt remained disaffected. The work of Justinian's successors, notably Heraclius, was also fruitless, the old hatreds remained unappeased, and finally the Churches of Armenia, Syria, and Egypt, still separate, passed under Moslem control. See Grégoire, *loc. cit.*, pp. 100–104. Note also Bark, *loc. cit.*, pp. 410–26.

80. See Otto G. von Simson, *Sacred Fortress. Byzantine Art and Statecraft in Ravenna* (Chicago, 1948), pp. 12–13, 20, for an account of the Western opposition to Justinian, particularly to his brutal treatment of Vigilius and to the pope's forced subservience to imperial policy.

81. Pirenne, *Mahomet*, pp. 54–55, 125, 191.

82. *Ibid.*, pp. 125–26.

83. After Justinian had at the beginning been dissuaded from undertaking the conquest of the Vandal kingdom, the dream of an Eastern bishop or perhaps an apparition of his own seems actually to have helped change his mind. See Stein, *Histoire du Bas-Empire*, II, 310, 312, and also J. B. Bury's cogent analysis of Justinian's policy, *History of the Later Roman Empire from the Death of Theodosius I to the Death of Justinian (A.D. 395 to A.D. 565)*, II (London, 1923), 26. Note the remark: "The resources of the state were not more than sufficient to protect the eastern frontier against the Persians and the Danubian against the barbarians of the north."

84. Bury, *A History of the Later Roman Empire from Arcadius to Irene (395 A.D. to 800 A.D.)*, I (London, 1889), 351. Stein, *Bas-Empire*, II, 276, would agree completely with the Janus image.

85. As Stein indicates (*Bas-Empire*, II, 310), Justinian regarded even the inadequate protection he gave the Balkan peninsula as an annoying restraint upon the vast projects to which he was devoted.

86. Bury, *Later Roman Empire*, I (1889), 352, and Stein, *Bas-Empire*, II,

277. See also Lot, FMA, pp. 298–321, whose chapters on the fate of Justinian's work are masterpieces of terse analysis.

87. For the quotation see Lot, FMA, p. 313.

88. Medievalists have long known and admired the stimulating interpretations of Alfons Dopsch as well as those of Henri Pirenne. Of basic importance is Dopsch's suggestion that a new Germanic culture was rising while the Roman was declining. See particularly "Vom Altertum zum Mittelalter: Das Kontinuitäts-problem," *Archiv für Kulturgeschichte,* XVI (1926), 159–82. The independence of the Germanic culture is exaggerated and the Germanic contribution *qua* Germanic is overdone, but, nevertheless, the idea that something new was coming into existence has much to recommend it. Aubin, *loc. cit.,* pp. 259–60, also stresses the German influence, perhaps a little too much. See also Erna Patzelt, *Die fränkische Kultur* (e.g., 64 ff.), a work which has not generally received the attention it deserves.

89. No one has expressed this better with special reference to the early Middle Ages than Christopher Dawson in his sensitive and keenly perceptive introduction to *The Making of Europe,* especially pp. xxi–xxiii. I cannot agree, however, that "the Catholic historian possesses an obvious advantage" in interpreting medieval culture; one might as well argue that the Marxist historian is best qualified to interpret the significance of Communism in the modern world. As for the difficulty men of a later age have in understanding values of men of an earlier age, it would be hard to find a better statement than that of C. H. McIlwain in his presidential address, "The Historian's Part in a Changing World," *American Historical Review,* XLII (1937), 207–24, especially pp. 211–13.

90. As usual, the difference between East and West has to be carefully drawn. The essential distinction is that Christianity in the West operated in a simple and almost unformed society, that it had a freer hand. I believe that is one important reason why the medieval West so far surpassed the Byzantine East in inventiveness. In relation to the development of later Western civilization medieval civilization is the fountainhead, whereas the Byzantine, rich, brilliant, and magnificent though it was, served rather as a rampart and a storehouse. Certainly Christianity had much to fight against in the East beside the Moslems, viz., a strongly established governmental system, an arrogant nobility, great wealth and grandeur. The existence side by side of the softest luxury and harsh asceticism, of cold cynicism and ardent faith, of squalid corruption and pure devotion, made it a civilization of contradictions hardly comparable with the medieval Western.

NOTES TO CHAPTER III

1. Cf. Paul Vinogradoff, "Social and Economic Conditions of the Roman Empire in the Fourth Century," *Cambridge Medieval History,* I (1924), 544.

2. For Rostovtzeff's views see preferably *The Social and Economic History of the Roman Empire,* particularly pp. 468–87; the quotation is from p. 477.

3. Lot, FMA, p. 19, and Rostovtzeff, *Social and Economic History,* pp. 464 ff.

4. *Ibid.,* p. 478.

5. Lot, FMA, pp. 33 ff., and Rostovtzeff, *Social and Economic History,* p. 456. There are now a good many opinions on this point, several of very recent origin.

6. Lot, FMA, pp. 12–13. Cf. the view of Ernst Stein, *Geschichte des spätrömischen Reiches.* I. *Vom römischen zum byzantinischen Staate (284–476 n. Chr.)* (Vienna, 1928), p. 337, that in reality there had been division from the time of Diocletian.

7. Lot, FMA, p. 44. Cf. Stein, *Spätrömisches Reich,* pp. 2–3, on the relatively greater importance of Diocletian's work in shifting the capital away from Rome to the East. It will be evident that I am not departing from my earlier statement that the Roman regression was not a misfortune. Too abrupt a collapse of Roman power and culture would have been very harmful to the development of Christian civilization. See for the survival of the idea of Empire, Robert Folz, *L'Idée de l'Empire en Occident du Ve au XIVe siècle* (Paris, 1953), pp. 11–18.

8. Bury, *Later Roman Empire* (1889), I, 1.

9. Stein, *Spätrömisches Reich,* p. 3; and on Gaul, Piganiol, *L'Empire chrétien,* pp. 1–2.

10. See Demougeot, *De l'Unité à la division de l'Empire romain,* pp. 532 ff., on the economic decline of the Western regions at the beginning of the fifth century.

11. Gunnar Mickwitz, "Le Problème de l'or dans le monde antique," *Annales d'histoire économique et sociale,* VI (1934), 246, disposes of the old view, derived from the Elder Pliny, that the reason for the scarcity of gold and silver coinage was the draining away of vast quantities of the precious metals to the Indies. According to this view, the scarcity of metal for use as money was connected with the rise of natural economy. The old arguments seem naïve enough in the light of more recent knowledge. For a comment from a somewhat different point of view, however, see Marc Bloch, "Le Problème de l'or au moyen âge," *Annales d'histoire économique et sociale,* V (1933), 11. Cf. Lot, FMA, p. 513, who would no doubt agree with Mickwitz rather than Bloch in this particular. Much remains to be done on this subject.

12. Note that Bloch and Mickwitz in the two articles just cited (*Annales d'histoire économique et sociale,* V (1933), 24; VI (1934), 241), writing during the Depression, made a somewhat similar comparison. Bloch comments on the influence of the richer Byzantine and Islamic economies upon that of the West; Mickwitz on the third-century preference for gold coin rather than silver, as indicated in hoards.

13. Stein, *Spätrömisches Reich,* pp. 21–22, 24.

14. *Ibid.,* pp. 23, 520–21, and Gunnar Mickwitz, *Geld und Wirtschaft im römischen Reich des vierten Jahrhunderts n. Chr.,* Societas Scientiarum Fennicæ Commentationes Humanarum Litterarum, Vol. IV, No. 2 (Helsingfors, 1932), p. 189. For the sums extracted by Attila see Johannes Sundwall, *Weströmisch Studien* (Berlin, 1915), pp. 153–54.

15. Stein, *Spätrömisches Reich,* pp. 23 (n. 3), 508–11.

16. As Arnaldo Momigliano points out in a review of Pirenne's *Mohammed and Charlemagne* and of R. S. Lopez's "Mohammed and Charlemagne: A Revision," *loc. cit.*, in *The Journal of Roman Studies*, XXXIV (1944), 157, the probability that the number of Syrians and Jews increased in Gaul in the early fifth century does not alter the evidence for the late fifth and the sixth centuries and does not prove that Jews and Syrians had come directly from the East. The subject is referred to again below. Note also the views of Solomon Katz, *The Jews in the Visigothic and Frankish Kingdoms of Spain and Gaul* (Cambridge, Mass., 1937), pp. 125–36.

17. For the presence, colonies, and methods of the Oriental merchants see Stein, *Spätrömisches Reich,* p. 26; Demougeot, *De l'Unité à la division de l'Empire romain,* pp. 534–35; and Salin, *Civilisation mérovingienne,* pp. 143–51.

18. Piganiol, *L'Empire chrétien,* pp. 294–96.

19. *Ibid.,* p. 296.

20. See also the interesting speculations of Lot, FMA, pp. 513–14.

21. Piganiol, *L'Empire chrétien,* p. 298; Lot, FMA, pp. 514–15. Concerning the *solidus* see Piganiol, pp. 295–96; Stein, *Spätrömisches Reich,* pp. 177–78; and Mickwitz, *Geld und Wirtschaft,* p. 77.

22. See Mickwitz, *Geld und Wirtschaft,* pp. 1–17, for a discussion of the meaning of natural and money economy and their historical significance in the fourth century. The author considers the views of a good many historians and economists on this subject, among others Hildebrand, Bücher, Meyer, Rostovtzeff, Pirenne, Dopsch, Persson, Stein, Sombart, and Heckscher.

23. For further definition see Alfons Dopsch, "Naturalwirtschaft und Geldwirtschaft in der Weltgeschichte," in *Beiträge zur Sozial- und Wirtschaftsgeschichte* (Vienna, 1938), p. 85. Dopsch is doubtless right, when he says (p. 86) that even in the lowest stages of development there was no closed house-economy in Bücher's sense. It is essential in the definition of a self-sufficient economy to note, first, that it *can* be self-sufficient and, second, that it is as self-sufficient as it is because it has to be. Clearly in simple societies there would be little opportunity for free exchange. There would be exchange rather of whatever commodities were available, which would mean restricted rather than free exchange. As Werner Sombart, "Economic Theory and Economic History," *Economic History Review,* II (1929), 13, says in arguing against Hildebrand's division of economic development into stages, "The contrast which demands emphasis is not that between the natural and the money economy but that between the economy which is self-sufficing and the economy which is not." Note here, and earlier, especially pp. 1–7, his castigation of the historians of things economic for what he regards as stereotyped thinking.

24. There were of course wide variations of conditions within the Empire, and what went on in one part at any given time did not of necessity go on in all the other parts. See Rostovtzeff, "The Decay of the Ancient World and Its Economic Explanations," *loc. cit.,* 200–201.

25. According to Mickwitz, *Geld und Wirtschaft*, p. 167, n. 4, there is no authentic evidence of payment in kind before Diocletian. Presumably the introduction of the practice was suggested by the bureaucracy, since it worked to their advantage. Generally disturbed conditions, including the status of money, would have prepared the way for the innovation. See further, *ibid.*, pp. 175–78. In the preceding pages Mickwitz presents a careful study of *adaeratio* in connection with payments and tax collections in kind. See also Lot, "Un Grand Domaine à l'époque franque. Ardin en Poitou, contribution à l'étude de l'impôt," in *Bibliothèque de l'école des hautes études,* fasc. 230 (Paris, 1921), pp. 122 ff., and *Nouvelles Recherches sur l'impôt foncier,* pp. 56 ff.

26. Lot, FMA, p. 65.

27. *Ibid.*, pp. 64–65.

28. *Ibid.*, pp. 66–67. On the relationship of the whole struggle between large landowners and small farmers with the development of a feudal type of society and its meaning for a monarchical government, see M. Rostowzew (Rostovtzeff), *Studien zur Geschichte des römischen Kolonates* (Leipzig and Berlin, 1910), p. 398.

29. Stein, *Spätrömisches Reich,* p. 23, and Piganiol, *L'Empire chrétien,* p. 299. Cf. Mickwitz, *Geld und Wirtschaft,* pp. 2–4.

30. Demougeot, *De l'Unité à la division,* pp. 505–10; Lot, FMA, p. 514; and Stein, *Spätrömisches Reich,* pp. 26–27.

31. Mickwitz, *Geld und Wirtschaft,* p. 176.

32. *Ibid.*, p. 166.

33. *Ibid.*, pp. 167–78.

34. See Mickwitz's whole discussion of the question of *adaeratio, ibid.*, pp. 165–78, including his tables based on the imperial laws in the Theodosian Code, pp. 170–73.

35. Angelo Segrè, "The Byzantine Colonate," *Traditio,* V (1947), 122 f., and Francis de Zulueta, "De Patrociniis Vicorum, a Commentary on C. Th. 11, 24 and C. J. 11, 54," in *Oxford Studies in Social and Legal History,* I (Oxford, 1909), 14–17. Both works are concerned primarily with the East but contain valuable information on the institution of the colonate in general. See also Paul Vinogradoff, "Social and Economic Conditions of the Roman Empire in the Fourth Century," *Cambridge Medieval History,* I (1924), 558 ff., and Rostovtzeff, *Geschichte des römischen Kolonates,* pp. 398 f.

36. Marc Bloch, "The Rise of Dependent Cultivation and Seigniorial Institutions," *Cambridge Economic History,* I (1941), 244, and Maurice Pallasse, *Orient et Occident à propos du colonat romain au Bas-Empire* (Paris, 1950), pp. 5-12.

37. Mickwitz, *Geld und Wirtschaft,* pp. 179–80. For other opinions on this topic, see Pallasse's comments on the studies of Angelo Segrè, Gino Segrè, and Charles Saumagne, pp. 6–8. For a critique of Saumagne's views and those of P. Collinet, see Stein, *Bas-Empire,* p. 208 n. Note also Rostovtzeff, *Geschichte*

des römischen Kolonates, pp. 397 ff., for some unusually interesting interpretations, and for another indication of the difficulty of deciphering the economic evidence see Robert P. Blake, "The Monetary Reform of Anastasius I and Its Economic Implications," in *Studies in the History of Culture,* published for the Conference of Secretaries of the American Council of Learned Societies (Menasha, Wis., 1942), pp. 84–97.

38. This the emperors fully realized, as shown, for example, by the expressed opposition of Anastasius I to the enslavement of free men, Stein, *Bas-Empire,* p. 207.

39. As Mickwitz indicates, *Geld und Wirtschaft,* pp. 184 ff., the proprietor suffered not only from losing the rent owed him by the runaway *coloni* but also from losing their labor, which was difficult to replace.

40. Mickwitz, *Geld und Wirtschaft,* p. 185.

41. Lot, FMA, pp. 140–42.

42. Mickwitz, *Geld und Wirtschaft,* p. 186.

43. See also Mickwitz's remarks, *ibid.,* pp. 187–88.

44. Piganiol, *L'Empire chrétien,* pp. 299–300.

45. Lot, FMA, p. 514.

46. Cf. Baynes in his review of Lot, FMA, in *Journal of Roman Studies,* XIX (1929), 228.

47. Sundwall, *Weströmische Studien,* pp. 153 f.

48. Mickwitz, *Geld und Wirtschaft,* pp. 144–46, 185–86, and Edward R. Hardy, *The Large Estates of Byzantine Egypt* (New York, 1931), pp. 50–51, 73–74, 100–101. On patronage and the colonate in Egypt, see also Allan C. Johnson and Louis C. West, *Byzantine Egypt: Economic Studies* (Princeton, 1949), pp. 22–29, 47 ff.

49. Bury, *Later Roman Empire* (1923), I, 441–46, and Stein, *Bas-Empire,* pp. 210 ff., 479 f.

50. Hardy, *Large Estates,* pp. 15–24, on the general state of Byzantine Egypt; also pp. 50–51, 75–76.

51. Albert Stöckle, *Spätrömische und byzantinische Zünfte, Klio,* Beiheft 9 (Leipzig, 1911), pp. 138–41, indicates that this was so in the tenth century. Presumably, and for the same reasons as in the tenth century, it was so long before.

52. Mickwitz, *Geld und Wirtschaft,* p. 188.

53. See, for example, Stöckle, *Zünfte,* p. 139, and Mickwitz, *Geld und Wirtschaft,* p. 145.

54. Sundwall, *Weströmische Studien,* pp. 160–61.

55. *Philosophiae consolatio* I, iv, ll. 34–49. On the other hand, the *tenuiores,* the small landowners, sometimes welcomed barbarian rulers, because even if their status was no better than before, they no longer had to pay the heavy costs of Roman government and army; see Courtenay E. Stevens, "Agriculture and Rural Life in the Later Roman Empire," *Cambridge Economic History,* I (1944),

117. It is also true that Theodoric and Totila, like some of their imperial predecessors in Italy, attempted to protect the small farmer from the oppression of the powerful. Can we believe, however, that the Goths would finally have been any more successful than Roman and Byzantine rulers, who had equally good reasons for controlling the landlords? See Dopsch, "Agrarian Institutions of the Germanic Kingdoms from the Fifth to the Ninth Centuries," and Georg Ostrogorsky, "Agrarian Conditions in the Byzantine Empire in the Middle Ages," *Cambridge Economic History,* I, 171, 195.

56. Sundwall, *Weströmische Studien,* p. 161. The existence of money in Italy is not in question. Sundwall shows (pp. 154–61) that in the fifth century the senatorial aristocracy possessed great wealth. The important point is that there was not enough wealth, and that the State could not even control those who owned what there was.

57. Cf. Piganiol, *L'Empire chrétien,* pp. 300, 417; Piganiol, of course, would not agree.

58. Norman Baynes, "The Decline of the Roman Power in Western Europe. Some Modern Explanations," *Journal of Roman Studies,* XXXIII (1943), 34–35, argues succinctly that the poverty of the Western Empire made impossible the maintenance of the civil and military system which the ancient civilization required for continued existence.

59. What Mickwitz, *Geld und Wirtschaft,* pp. 190–91, says in his conclusion is that the doctrine of a "dominant" natural economy in the fourth century can no longer be maintained. He proceeds to point out, however, that State finances were an exception, that here a system of natural economy held sway, and that the *raison d'être* of this remarkable phenomenon in an economy in other respects based on gold is to be sought in the social relationships of the time. The rest of his conclusions, to which I shall refer before long, are, if anything, even more damaging to Pirenne's position.

60. Baynes, review of Lot, Pirenne, and Rostovtzeff, in *Journal of Roman Studies,* XIX (1929), 230.

61. *Ibid.,* pp. 231 ff.

62. Gunnar Mickwitz, "Der Verkehr auf dem westlichen Mittelmeer um 600 n. Chr.," in *Wirtschaft und Kultur. Festschrift zum 70. Geburtstag von Alfons Dopsch* (Baden bei Wien, Leipzig, 1938), pp. 74–83. Cf. Archibald R. Lewis, "Le Commerce et la navigation sur les côtes atlantiques de la Gaule du Ve au VIIIe siècle," *Le Moyen Âge,* LIX (1953), 247–98.

63. Marc Bloch, review of Rudolf Buchner, *Die Provence in merowingischer Zeit. Verfassung-Wirtschaft-Kultur* (Stuttgart, 1933), in *Annales d'histoire économique et sociale,* VI (1934), 188–89.

64. Marc Bloch, "Le Problème de l'or au moyen âge," *loc. cit.,* pp. 7–8.

65. *Ibid.,* pp. 8–9. See also Dennett, *loc. cit.,* p. 188, and his citations of Maurice Prou and Bloch. Cf. Perroy, *loc. cit.,* pp. 232–33.

66. Bloch, "Le Problème de l'or," *loc. cit.,* pp. 9–10.

67. *Ibid.*, pp. 10–11. A year later in a review already cited, *Annales,* VI (1934), 188–89, Bloch indicated more clearly, though still with the greatest consideration, his doubts about this aspect of Pirenne's interpretation. Note also Mlle Demougeot's observation (*De l'Unité à la division,* pp. 535 f.) that if it is necessary to put off until the Arabic invasions the beginning of medieval commerce, "as W. Heyd, A. Schaube, and H. Pirenne have shown," it is no less true that the Roman West abruptly passed into a state of decadence after 410. And of course the monetary policy of the Western Empire altered in accordance with the economic decline. As she remarks, most mints fell into barbarian hands at this time; it was only to be expected that barbarian kings would continue to stamp coins with the effigies of the emperors. Far from attesting the persistence of the economic unity of the Empire, as Pirenne says (*Mahomet,* p. 89), the fact that *barbarian kings* struck these coins attests its political and economic disunity. Consider also the practice of medieval European rulers and even bishops, in the eleventh and twelfth centuries as well as earlier, of striking coins of foreign pattern, including the Moslem, and copying their models even in such details as Arabic words and citations from the Koran. See Bloch, "Le Problème de l'or," *loc. cit.*, pp. 19 ff. This extensive use of foreign rather than indigenous coin patterns does not indicate that Western rulers were "united" with the Moslems any more than the German rulers were "united" with the Eastern Empire in an earlier time. I suggest that in both cases we have instances of weaker economies showing their respect for stronger economies by copying their outward tokens and thus trying to insure greater stability of values in exchange. In both cases it was recognized that the value of money rests upon confidence. Again this practice resembles the modern usage, prevalent in many parts of the world, by which values are represented in dollars even in places where genuine American dollars rarely, if ever, appear. In connection with this last point, note Bloch's interesting comparison, *loc. cit.*, p. 24. Bloch's case for the use of foreign coin patterns is subject to debate.

68. Mickwitz, "Le Problème de l'or dans l'antiquité," *loc. cit.*, p. 247.

69. Bloch, "Le Problème de l'or," *loc. cit.*, p. 12.

70. Dennett, *loc. cit.*, pp. 187 ff. Note also Bloch's comment, "Le Problème de l'or," *loc. cit.*, p. 18, that most European exports, to the extent that these continued, were to Islamic countries, especially to Spain, and that the rupture provoked by the Moslem invasions was not complete. See Latouche, *Les Origines de l'économie,* pp. 154 ff.

71. Note also his rejection of Lot's evidence in support of the view that natural economy prevailed in the Merovingian epoch, *Mahomet,* p. 96, n. 1.

72. Mickwitz, *Geld und Wirtschaft,* pp. 2–3, 190.

73. *Ibid.*, pp. 4, 189.

74. *Ibid.*, pp. 190–91.

75. I have already called attention to Pirenne's citation (*Mahomet,* p. 89, n. 4) of Mickwitz's belief that the fourth century cannot be considered a period

of natural economy. The inadequacy of this citation accompanied by no mention of Mickwitz's views about natural economy in State finances and the results thereof will be obvious.

76. Mickwitz, *Geld und Wirtschaft,* p. 189.

77. *Ibid.,* p. 191.

78. For example, by Lot, FMA, p. 213, and Mickwitz, *Geld und Wirtschaft,* p. 188–89.

79. This has been trenchantly expressed by Albert de Broglie, *L'Église et l'Empire romain au IVe siècle,* 2d ed., II (Paris, 1857), 228–29. Lot quite properly and generously renders homage to his predecessor, FMA, pp. 97–98.

80. Lot, FMA, pp. 256, 261.

81. For Jerome's feelings see *Ep.* 126, 2; 127, 12; 128, 5; and *Com. in Ezech.* 1 pref. and 3 pref. On the general reaction and the views of other contemporaries, see L. Duchesne, *Histoire ancienne de l'église,* III (Paris, 1911), 193, and Labriolle, *Histoire de la littérature latine chrétienne,* pp. 580 ff. Consult also Johannes Straub, "Christliche Geschichtsapologetik in der Krisis des römischen Reiches," *Historia,* I (1950), 52–81, which contains numerous references to recent German contributions, several of which have not been available to me. Johannes Geffcken's essay, "Stimmungen im untergehenden Weströmerreich," *Neue Jahrbücher für das klassische Altertum, Geschichte und deutsche Literatur,* XXIII (1920), 256–69, which is also a stimulating piece of work, does not give specific citations.

82. On this subject see Angelo Segrè, *loc. cit.,* pp. 128–30, and Albert Grenier, *La Gaule romaine,* in *An Economic Survey of Ancient Rome* (ed. Tenney Frank), III (Baltimore, 1937). In his sixth chapter, "Le Bas-Empire," Grenier quotes at length from the panegyrists and others.

83. Note particularly his remark that the "Romana respublica," if not already dead, is certainly dying in that region in which it still seems to have some life, being choked to death by taxes, *De gubernatione Dei,* IV, 30 [(ed. Franz Pauly), *Corpus Scriptorum Ecclesiasticorum Latinorum,* VIII (Vienna, 1883)]. References to this work will hereafter be given in parentheses in the body of the text. See also Stein, *Spätrömisches Reich,* pp. 511–12. For a much less friendly view of Salvian's worth see Pierre Courcelle, *Histoire littéraire des grandes invasions germaniques* (Paris, 1948), pp. 126–27, though perhaps the French scholar, because of the time when he wrote, was a little too suspicious of Salvian. Cf. his remarks on the "Occupation" in the *Avant-propos.* Note also Laistner, *Thought and Letters,* pp. 74–75, and André Loyen, *Sidoine Apollinaire et l'esprit précieux en Gaule aux derniers jours de l'Empire* (Paris, 1943), pp. 52 f.

84. Lot, FMA, p. 148.

85. Sidonius Apollinaris, *Carmina,* XII (ed. W. B. Anderson), in the Loeb Classical Library (Cambridge, Mass., 1936), also makes some disdainful remarks about the personal manners of the Germans. Cf. Loyen, *Sidoine Apollinaire,* pp. 52 f., and *Recherches historiques sur les panégyriques de Sidoine Apollinaire,*

Fasc. 285 of the *Bibliothèque de l'École des hautes études,* Sciences historiques et philologiques (Paris, 1942), pp. 13 ff. In this introduction, Loyen presents a lively picture of Sidonius' Gaul.

86. Cf. R. Thouvenot, "Salvien et la ruine de l'Empire romain," *École française de Rome. Mélanges d'archéologie et d'histoire,* XXXVII (1918–19), 152–53.

87. *Ibid.,* p. 159.

88. Albert de Broglie, *L'Église et l'Empire,* pp. 228–29, points out vividly how long the decline had been going on before the fourth century.

Few observers of this period of history can have failed to ponder the fact that millions of Romans were vanquished by scores of thousands of Germans. According to Salvian, it was not by the natural strength of their bodies that the barbarians conquered, nor by the weakness of their nature that the Romans were defeated. It was the Romans' moral vices alone that overcame them (VII, 108). Narrow as it is, this judgment by one very close to the event remains respectable.

As for the men of more exalted position, the well-educated noblemen, who fled to the barbarians in order to escape the persecution and injustice that prevailed among the Romans (V, 21, 23), it is clear that they, like their poorer compatriots, had given up hope of obtaining justice and protection from the Roman state and its laws. Their flight confirms the fact that in large areas of the Western Empire public spirit and public justice had disappeared, and that men were obliged to act privately and locally in matters that had formerly been regulated by central governmental authority.

89. Paulus Orosius, *Historiarum adversum paganos libri vii* (ed. Karl F. W. Zangemeister), in *Corpus Scriptorum Ecclesiasticorum Latinorum* (Vienna, 1882), VII, 41, 7.

90. Sidonius Apollinaris, *Epistulae,* I, 2. With reference to the motive see Sir Samuel Dill, *Roman Society in the Last Century of the Western Empire,* 2d ed., revised (London, 1905), pp. 328–29.

91. Consider, for example, Dill's pertinent remarks, *ibid.,* pp. 262–63. It is interesting to note that Synesius in his letters, written not long before Salvian, found conditions in the East, though trying, still quite bearable. See also the fascinating proposals for reforms presented in the *De rebus bellicis* written by an anonymous writer probably of the fourth century, edited and translated by E. A. Thompson under the heading *A Roman Reformer and Inventor, Being a New Text of the Treatise "De rebus bellicis"* (Oxford, 1952). The amazing Anonymus, however, like Synesius, seems to have been more interested in the Eastern part of the Empire, and he was of course earlier than Salvian.

92. Note the restrictions and limitations imposed by François Ganshof, *Feudalism,* tr. Philip Grierson (London, 1952), pp. xv–xviii. The edition cited is the first English edition, based on the second French edition but with numerous corrections and additions.

93. Robert S. Smith, "Medieval Agrarian Society in Its Prime. Section 3. Spain," *Cambridge Economic History,* I, 345.

94. According to Arnold J. Toynbee, *A Study of History,* I (London, 1934), 19 (p. 2 of the abridged edition, New York and London, 1947), "Vinogradoff has brilliantly demonstrated that the seeds of it [the feudal system] had already sprouted on English soil before the Norman Conquest." Of Vinogradoff's brilliance there is no question, but there is some difference of opinion about his interpretation of this point. For an excellent account which gives a clear description of the opposing interpretations developed by some of the ablest British, American, and continental specialists over the last half century, see Carl Stephenson, "Feudalism and Its Antecedents in England," *American Historical Review,* XLVIII (1943), 245–65. For the present discussion the significance of the controversy over the state of pre-Norman England with respect to feudalism is that it clearly shows that feudalism by any strict definition was not universal in Western Europe during the Middle Ages. Whether we regard English government before the Conquest as feudal or prefeudal, it differed in some important respects from that of France. Yet both governments were localized and oligarchic, both lands relied upon a type of agricultural production generally called seigniorial, and both were "medieval" in culture.

95. For recognition of the importance of this subject we have primarily to thank Ludo M. Hartmann, who presents it forcefully in his little study *Ein Kapitel vom spätantiken und frühmittelalterlichen Staate* (Berlin, 1913), which Norman Baynes justly praised in his review of Lot's *La Fin du monde antique, Journal of Roman Studies,* XIX (1929), 226.

96. Hartmann, *Ein Kapitel,* pp. 10–11. See also Wilhelm Ensslin, "The Emperor and the Imperial Administration," in *Byzantium* (ed. Baynes and Moss), pp. 274–75. There were limitations, however, especially in doctrinal matters. Cf. *ibid.,* pp. 275–76; Norman Baynes's Introduction, pp. xxviii–xxix; and Henri Grégoire, "The Byzantine Church," pp. 130 ff. With reference to the financial system see André M. Andréadès, "Public Finances: Currency, Public Expenditure, Budget, Public Revenue," *ibid.,* pp. 84–85; and on the bureaucracy and military matters, Ensslin, *ibid.,* pp. 280 ff., 294, 302 ff. Cf. Werner Ohnsorge, *Das Zweikaiserproblem im früheren Mittelalter. Die Bedeutung des byzantinischen Reiches für die Entwicklung der Staatsidee in Europa* (Hildesheim, 1947), pp. 7–15.

97. Hartmann, *Ein Kapitel,* pp. 13–14; Lot, *Les Destinées,* p. 305; Ganshof, *Les Destinées,* p. 228.

98. Hartmann in *Ein Kapitel* consistently speaks of the natural economy of the West as contrasted with the money economy of the East. Mickwitz points out (*Geld und Wirtschaft,* p. 3) that Meyer and Rostovtzeff agreed with Bücher in this, if in nothing else, that the fourth century was economically a transition period·to the Middle Ages and that its economy was very close to natural economy. The reader will be aware that the whole question has stirred up much

controversy, that Mickwitz had his own modifications to offer, and that from the fourth century the economic systems of East and West tended to diverge more and more sharply.

99. It will be worth stating once more at this point Sombart's observation, "Economic Theory and Economic History," *loc. cit.*, p. 13, that "the contrast which demands emphasis is not that between the natural and the money economy but that between the economy which is self-sufficing and the economy which is not."

100. So Hartmann, *Ein Kapitel*, pp. 5–6, 13, would interpret it. Note also Mickwitz's observation (*Geld und Wirtschaft*, p. 188) that the bondage inseparable from all systems of natural economy brought about the same result in antiquity and the Middle Ages: the Privilege-State (*Privilegienstaat*). He makes the further point here that the Byzantine Empire did not have compulsory corporations, which underlines the difference between medieval East and West with respect to the use of repression. Hartmann strongly emphasizes the contrast between the repressive principle as applied in the West and the preventive as applied in the East, *Ein Kapitel*, pp. 16, 22.

101. *Ibid.*, pp. 11–12.

102. "The Decay of the Ancient World," *loc. cit.*, p. 198.

103. It is interesting to note that although Constantine's reign began shortly after the beginning of the fourth century and the able Theodosius I died shortly before the century's end, for the Roman imperial government conditions had deteriorated badly by 395. It was the battle of Adrianople, after all, that brought Theodosius to the throne, and Alaric's capture of Rome occurred only fifteen years after Theodosius' death. Many of the measures that won Theodosius the title of greatness, moreover, were required by a wise recognition of the Empire's feebleness. The recovery ended with his reign, then, if not before. It is also noteworthy that he carried forward Constantine's policy of favoring the Christian Church. Cf. Straub, "Christliche Geschichtsapologetik," *loc. cit.*, pp. 55–56.

104. "The Decay of the Ancient World," *loc. cit.*, p. 198.

NOTES TO CHAPTER IV

1. *A Study of History*, I, 62 (in the abridged edition, p. 14).

2. For some interesting reflections on this question, avowing the strength of the Oriental influence, see Hans Lietzmann, "Das Problem der Spätantike," *Sitzungsberichte der preussischen Akademie der Wissenschaften*, Philosophisch-historische Klasse (1927), pp. 342–58, particularly the concluding remarks, pp. 357–58. I disagree with an observation made by Lot, FMA, p. 157. As Norman Baynes pointed out [*Journal of Roman Studies*, XIX (1929), 227], Lot, in holding that art came to an end in the fourth century, seems to imply that the Middle Ages had none. If this is what he meant, we should have before us another

example of the familiar point of view that when something ancient and pagan came to an end, all was over. No doubt he did not mean to go so far, but I must agree with Baynes that Lot here slighted the subject and passed over several interesting problems connected with it. It is puzzling to note (cf. Baynes, *loc. cit.,* p. 227, n. 2) that later on (FMA, pp. 170–71) Lot takes a different position, actually concluding, "Ainsi, dans le domaine de l'art, comme dans celui de la religion, au IVe siècle, une âme nouvelle se substitue à l'âme antique." So all was not over after all. See also the résumé of Jean Hubert's paper, "Quelques Sources de l'art carolingien," *Settimane di studio,* I, 215–19, and Charles R. Morey, *Mediaeval Art* (New York, 1942), p. 188. Cf. the articles in *Settimane di studio,* III, *I Goti in Occidente: Problemi* (Spoleto, 1956), especially Carlo Cecchelli, "Motivi orientali e occidentali nell'arte del periodo dei Goti in Italia," pp. 43–55, and Pedro Palol de Salellas, "Esencia del arte hispanico de época visigoda: Romanismo y germanismo," pp. 65–126, and the "Discussione" of this paper, pp. 131–34.

3. Studies of St. Augustine's views on salvation and scientific knowledge are very numerous and very well known. For outstanding recent interpretations of them, see Charles N. Cochrane, *Christianity and Classical Culture. A Study of Thought and Action from Augustus to Augustine* (Toronto, 1944), pp. 450–55, and Henri-Irénée Marrou, *Saint-Augustin et la fin de la culture antique* (Paris, 1938), pp. 234–35.

4. Cf. *ibid.,* pp. 352 ff.

5. For a brief recent consideration of leading Christian views, especially before 410, see Theodor Mommsen, "St. Augustine and the Christian Idea of Progress," *Journal of the History of Ideas,* XII (1951), 346–74. Note also Straub, "Christliche Geschichtsapologetik," *loc. cit.,* pp. 52–81, and Geffcken, "Stimmungen im untergehenden Weströmerreich," *loc. cit.,* pp. 256–69.

6. On Eusebius and others who agreed with him, such as John Chrysostom, Ambrose, Jerome, Cyril of Alexandria, and Theodoret of Cyrus, see Mommsen, *loc. cit.,* pp. 362 ff.

7. Cf. Straub, "Christliche Geschichtsapologetik," *loc. cit.,* pp. 62–63, and Mommsen, *loc. cit.,* pp. 367–68.

8. Cf. Straub, *loc. cit.,* p. 77.

9. It is particularly interesting to note that in his well-known story of Athaulf's intention to obliterate the Roman name and turn the Roman into a Gothic Empire, Orosius (VII, 43, 4–7) relates that the barbarian ruler also intended to make "Gothia" out of what had been "Romania." From the tenor of his language it appears that Orosius agreed with Athaulf's conclusion that because of the backwardness of the barbarians, this could not be done, at least not at that time. If nothing else, however, the story shows that the replacement of the Roman name, Empire, and culture was thought about and discussed. Cf. Straub, *loc. cit.,* p. 75, and Ottorino Bertolini, " 'Gothia' e 'Romania,' " *Settimane di studio,* III, 13–33.

10. It has been done by Mommsen, *loc. cit.,* especially pp. 369–74, and by Straub, *loc. cit.,* pp. 64–65, 69.

11. Mommsen, *loc. cit.,* p. 374.

12. Cf. Straub, *loc. cit.,* p. 71.

13. *Ibid.,* pp. 72, 78.

14. Edward Gibbon, *The History of the Decline and Fall of the Roman Empire* (ed. J. B. Bury), 5th ed. (London, 1923), V, 169.

15. Rostovtzeff, "The Decay of the Ancient World," *loc. cit.,* p. 199.

16. Dawson, *The Making of Europe,* p. 159.

17. See the interesting account given by Richard E. Sullivan in one of the most recent works published on this subject, "The Carolingian Missionary and the Pagan," *Speculum,* XXVIII (1953), 705–40, especially pp. 706, 726–28. Many works might be cited here, above all the letters of St. Boniface. See also René Aigrain, *Histoire de l'église depuis les origines jusqu'à nos jours,* V, *Grégoire le Grand, les états barbares et la conquête arabe (590–757)* (Paris, 1947), pp. 311 ff., 497 f., 526–42; Theodor Schieffer, *Winfrid-Bonifatius und die christliche Grundlegung Europas* (Freiburg im Breisgau, 1954), particularly on Boniface but also on the earlier work, pp. 41 ff., 52 ff., 60 ff.; Eleanor S. Duckett, *Anglo-Saxon Saints and Scholars* (New York, 1947), pp. 387 f., 391; George W. Greenaway, *Saint Boniface. Three Biographical Studies for the Twelfth Centenary Festival* (London, 1955), pp. 34 f., 40 ff.

18. Dawson, *The Making of Europe,* p. 154.

19. Sullivan, "The Carolingian Missionary," *loc. cit.,* pp. 732–33.

20. Much of the detailed information in this and the three preceding paragraphs is derived from the interesting and provocative paper "Early Medieval Missionary Activity: A Comparative Study," read on December 28, 1953, by Richard E. Sullivan at the session on "East and West in the Early Middle Ages" at the sixty-eighth annual meeting of the American Historical Association in Chicago, since published in a somewhat different form under the title "Early Medieval Missionary Activity: A Comparative Study of Eastern and Western Methods," *Church History,* XXIII (1954), 17–35. I have also profited from hearing and reading the other papers presented at this session, Gerhard B. Ladner's "The Idea of Reform in the Early Medieval East and West" and Carlo M. Cipolla's "Gold and Coins in the Mediterranean, ca. 400 to 900," and the comments prepared by Edward R. Hardy and A. R. Lewis. See also Margaret Deanesly, *A History of Early Medieval Europe, 476 to 911* (London, 1956), pp. 182 f.

21. A. R. Lewis, in a prepared comment read at the session on "East and West in the Early Middle Ages" referred to above, phrases it tellingly: ". . . when, in the 9th and 10th centuries, Carolingian Emperors, Anglo-Saxon rulers, and the Ottonian house in Germany re-established something like states in the West, the basic patterns of religious, economic and cultural life had already been established in response to organic social forces—not governmental pres-

sures. Since that time neither economic nor religious life in Western Christendom has ever been completely subservient to the state. Formed in freedom they have carried the seeds of this origin within them down to the present day."

22. Sullivan, "Early Medieval Missionary Activity," *loc. cit.,* p. 31.

23. Marc Bloch, *Les Caractères originaux de l'histoire rurale française,* new edition (Paris, 1952), p. x. The text and pagination are the same as in the 1931 edition. A second volume, a supplement prepared by Robert Dauvergne and published in 1956, presents Bloch's later views and revisions as indicated in articles and reviews published after the original Oslo edition. For appreciative notes on the value of Bloch's work, see Lucien Febvre's preface to the 1952 edition, pp. iii–vi, 7, and Lot's comment in FMA, pp. 517–18. My own great debt to Bloch's trail-blazing contributions in *Les Caractères,* in his later articles, and in his splendid chapter in the first volume of the *Cambridge Economic History* will be obvious in the pages that follow. This last work will hereafter be cited as CEH.

24. Marc Bloch, "The Rise of Dependent Cultivation and Seigniorial Institutions," CEH, I, 226–27.

25. *Ibid.,* p. 225.

26. See, for example, Charles Parain, "The Evolution of Agricultural Technique," CEH, I, 124 ff. Prosper Boissonade, *Life and Work in Medieval Europe (Fifth to Fifteenth Centuries),* translated by Eileen Power (New York, 1927), pp. 18 ff., 25 ff., 30–31, speaks of horrors and depredations perpetrated by the barbarians as if the invaders had seized a flourishing civilization and destroyed a prosperous and expanding economy. Cf. Courtenay E. Stevens, "Agricultural and Rural Life in the Later Roman Empire," CEH, I, 112 ff., on the state of the Late Roman economy.

27. Bloch, "The Rise of Dependent Cultivation," CEH, I, 226–27. See also *Les Caractères,* p. 67.

28. Bloch, *Les Caractères,* pp. 84, 161. The *seigneurie* was more than a piece of land worked by a group of peasants under the direction of a chief or lord. The term also implies authority based upon customary law, and this authority extended far beyond the economic realm. The lord's power of regulating the lives of his peasants supplemented, when it did not replace, that of the State. The *mansus,* as we see it in the medieval *seigneurie,* was the customary unit of tenure, though there were other kinds of holdings. Usually a *seigneurie* had both free and servile *mansi,* the servile being fewer in number, smaller, and more heavily burdened. Theoretically but not actually the *mansus* was an indivisible unit. See Bloch, "The Rise of Dependent Cultivation," CEH, I, 224–25, 230, 265, and also Lot's remarks, *Nouvelles Recherches, passim.* In addition to the works already cited on the development of feudalism, reference should be made to several articles in the *Settimane di studio,* I, *I problemi della civiltà carolingia* (Spoleto, 1954), and II, *I problemi comuni dell'Europa post carolingia* (Spoleto, 1955): especially François Ganshof, "L'Origine des rapports féodo-vassaliques:

les rapports féodo-vassaliques dans la monarchie franque au Nord des Alpes à l'époque carolingienne," I, 27–69; Pier Silverio Leicht, "Il Feudo in Italia nell'età carolingia," I, 71–107; and Claudio Sánchez-Albornoz, "Espana y el feudalismo carolingio. I: El prefeudalismo hispano-godo; II: Las instituciones feudales asturleonesas," I, 109–45. On the *mansus,* see further Roger Grand, "Les Moyens de résoudre dans le haut moyen âge les problèmes ruraux," *ibid.,* II, 523–46.

29. Bloch, *Les Caractères,* pp. 3–5.

30. Bloch, "The Rise of Dependent Cultivation," CEH, I, 235–39. Slaves remained more numerous in some places; e.g., there were many more in England during the century before the Conquest than on the continent, *ibid., p.* 258.

31. *Ibid., p.* 239.

32. For tenures akin to serfdom in the Later Empire, see Stevens, "Agriculture and Rural Life in the Later Roman Empire," CEH, I, 110 ff. For this and also for the fundamental importance of tenure with service after the *Völkerwanderung,* see Richard Koebner, "The Settlement and Colonisation of Europe," CEH, I, 32.

33. Bloch, "The Rise of Dependent Cultivation," CEH, I, 239.

34. *Ibid.,* pp. 241–43.

35. *Ibid.,* pp. 248 ff. Bloch also points out here that the granting of immunities had parallels almost everywhere, especially in Anglo-Saxon Britain.

36. *Ibid.,* pp. 250–51. (On the *ban* see also François Ganshof, "Medieval Agrarian Society in Its Prime," CEH, I, 315–16.) As Bloch points out (p. 251), many of the new rights claimed by lords from the tenth century on are called *banal* rights after the remote judicial right on which the lords based their claims to dues.

37. *Ibid., p.* 258.

38. *Ibid., p.* 255.

39. *Ibid., p.* 257.

40. *Ibid., p.* 248.

41. J. W. Thompson, "Serfdom in the Medieval Campagna," in the Dopsch-Festschrift already cited, pp. 380–81.

42. See, for example, Bloch, "The Rise of Dependent Cultivation," CEH, I, 275, on the small independent cultivators and the *livello.* See also Gino Luzzatto, *Storia economica d'Italia,* I (Rome, 1949), 147–50. Not only did certain parts of Italy differ from most of Europe, but there were differences within Italy. Note also Luzzatto's observation, *ibid.* pp. 144–45, concerning the Lombard invasions and the division of Italy with reference to Pirenne's views on the Arab conquest, and see his paper, "Mutamenti nell'economia agraria italiana dalla caduta dei carolingi al principio del sec. XI," *Settimane di studio,* II, 601–22, in which he often refers to the earlier period.

43. Bloch, CEH, I, 275, points out that the tax system established by the Romans in the provinces was not, at least not for a long time, applied in Italy.

44. *Ibid.*, pp. 265–68. Bloch of course brings in additional evidence. I am here referring only to that most pertinent to the subject of medieval origins.

45. *Ibid.*, pp. 262–64, but see also, on the origin and meaning of the *mansus,* Roger Grand, "Les Moyens de résoudre dans le haut moyen âge les les problèmes ruraux," in *Settimane di studio,* II, 523–46.

46. *Ibid.*, p. 272. Bloch, as indicated, has assembled considerable evidence, including place names, and has fortified his presentation by numerous and impressive appeals to comparative developments in other periods and places. See his whole discussion of chiefs and villages and his conclusions, *ibid.*, pp. 260–77, and also in *Les Caractères,* pp. 67, 77–81. See also Charles Verlinden, *L'Esclavage dans l'Europe médiévale,* Vol. I, *Péninsule ibérique-France* (Brugge, 1955), pp. 739, 743 ff.

47. Boissonade, *Life and Work,* pp. 18, 30; but see his whole account, pp. 17–31.

48. In connection with the Roman Peace one is reminded of the well-known words Tacitus (*Agricola,* 30) puts into the mouth of Calgacus, the outstanding chieftain of the Britons, to the effect that the Romans lie when they give the names of empire and peace to their brutal and destructive deeds: "Auferre trucidare rapere falsis nominibus imperium, atque ubi solitudinem faciunt, pacem appellant" ("Falsely do they call plunder, butchery, and rapine an Empire; where they make a desert, they call it peace"). As we know, many other Romans, both then and later (in the time of Alaric), did not think, or speak, so sarcastically of Roman accomplishments.

49. As Lynn White, Jr., remarks in "Technology and Invention in the Middle Ages," *Speculum,* XV (1940), 151, "Evidence is accumulating to show that a serf in the turbulent and insecure tenth century enjoyed a standard of living considerably higher than that of a proletarian in the reign of Augustus." Note the trenchant remarks of Grand on the values of the new social and economic system, "Les Moyens de résoudre . . . les problèmes ruraux," *loc. cit.*, II, 543 ff.

50. I shall here attempt only a sketch of the main discoveries and possibilities and their meaning for the problem of medieval beginnings. The volume of writings on this subject is already very large. For a useful note and references on the "problème Lefebvre des Noëttes," see Marc Bloch, "Les 'Inventions' médiévales," *Annales,* VII (1935), 634 and also Lynn White, Jr., "Technology and Invention in the Middle Ages," *loc. cit.*, pp. 153–54. Bloch has contributed much to the elucidation of the subject and its social implications, often in *Annales* but in other journals as well and in *Les Caractères.* White's lively and informative article, to which I also owe much, is itself a pioneer work in this country and provides rich and extensive bibliographical references. Lefebvre des Noëttes' chief work is *L'Attelage et le cheval de selle à travers les âges. Contribution à l'histoire de l'esclavage* (Paris, 1931), which in its earlier and smaller form (1924) was called *La Force motrice animale à travers les âges.* In addition to numerous shorter studies he also published *De la Marine antique à la marine*

moderne. La révolution du gouvernail. Contribution à l'étude de l'esclavage (Paris, 1935), which has less importance for the early medieval problem. See also Dauvergne, "Supplément" [to Bloch, *Les Caractères*], pp. 76–78, 141–43.

51. As Marc Bloch observed in a review of *La Force motrice animale* entitled "Technique et évolution sociale. A propos de l'histoire de l'attelage, et de celle de l'esclavage," *Revue de synthèse historique,* XLI (1926), 91, if the reflection stirred by Lefebvre des Noëttes' findings does not always and in every point confirm his conclusions, that is a fate escaped only by works which, devoid of ideas, suggest nothing at all. In "La Force motrice animale et le rôle des inventions techniques," *Revue de synthèse historique,* XLIII (1927), 83–91, Lefebvre des Noëttes answers certain of Bloch's criticisms and Bloch in turn replies to the Commandant's objections. I cite the article here not alone for its content, which is more than interesting, but as an outstanding example of the politeness of princes in the delicate work of criticism and response.

52. Émile Mâle, *La Fin du paganisme en Gaule et les plus anciennes basiliques chrétiennes* (Paris, 1950), pp. 317–20, 324.

53. *Ibid.,* pp. 320–24.

54. *Ibid.,* pp. 326 f.

55. In saying this, I do not have Toynbee's theory of challenge and response in mind, as I shall make clear elsewhere.

56. Lefebvre des Noëttes, "La Force motrice animale," *loc. cit.,* p. 84.

57. As Jakob Burckhardt remarked in his famous chapter "Die geschichtlichen Krisen," *Weltgeschichtliche Betrachtungen* (Berlin and Stuttgart, 1910), p. 165, it is not at all necessary—just as it is not in the barbarian invasions of Rome—to prophesy that rejuvenation will always emerge from destruction. See also his further comments on the great Roman disaster (especially pp. 168 ff.), which he regarded as a real crisis because it meant the fusion of a new material force with an old one, which, become a Church instead of a State, survived in an intellectual metamorphosis.

58. On the ancient Oriental, note Mâle, p. 327.

59. Cf. White, "Technology and Invention," *loc. cit.,* pp. 143–49.

60. *Ibid.,* pp. 143–44.

61. As Bloch suggests, "Les 'Inventions' médiévales," *loc. cit.,* p. 637.

62. See Jules Sion, "Quelques Problèmes de transports dans l'antiquité: le point de vue d'un géographe méditerranéen," *Annales,* VII, 628–33; note particularly Sion's conclusions.

63. Lefebvre des Noëttes, *L'Attelage,* pp. 9–17. See also Parain, "The Evolution of Agricultural Technique," CEH, I, 134, and Grand, *L'Agriculture,* pp. 444 f.

64. Lefebvre des Noëttes, *L'Attelage,* pp. 121–25 and Fig. 145.

65. *Ibid.,* p. 122. He attributed the invention of the horseshoe to the ninth century (p. 145).

66. *Ibid.*, pp. 15–17, 122–23.

67. Actually more than half-strangled if the weights that can be pulled by horses harnessed by the ancient and by the medieval systems are any indication. A team equipped with the rigid horse collar has been found capable of pulling three or four times as great a weight. See White, "Technology and Invention," *loc. cit.*, p. 154, and Lefebvre des Noëttes, *L'Attelage*, p. 123.

68. *Ibid.*, pp. 14–16, 122–23.

69. *Ibid.*, p. 12, for example.

70. André-G. Haudricourt, "De l'Origine de l'attelage moderne," *Annales*, VIII (1936) 515–22. For Lefebvre des Noëttes' views on the source of the stirrup and saddle, see *L'Attelage*, pp. 235–37.

71. Grand, *L'Agriculture*, pp. 446–49.

72. Indeed, Haudricourt, *loc. cit.*, p. 521, points to the possibility that increased land commerce in Eastern Europe, due to the use of the new harness, stimulated the maritime commerce of the Baltic and thereby the Norman expansion. Grand, *L'Agriculture*, pp. 446–48, mentions that Lefebvre des Noëttes found the Chinese of the Han Dynasty in possession of a breast collar. Though he acknowledges the possibility that this could have been carried across the Siberian and Russian steppes to be copied by the Scandinavians and Finns, he still presents his own theory of independent invention by the Laplanders as more acceptable.

73. Bloch, "Les 'Inventions' médiévales," *loc. cit.*, p. 640. I have not been able to consult the article by Roger Grand here cited by Bloch (p. 640, n. 2), but see Grand, *L'Agriculture*, p. 444, n. 1, and Lefebvre des Noëttes, *L'Attelage*, p. 125.

74. For the manuscript see Lefebvre des Noëttes, *L'Attelage*, p. 123. Note also that the earlier date would weaken Grand's hypothesis on the coincidence of the appearance of the new harness just after the settlement of the Normans in France and the Danish raids across the Channel. It is also provocative of thought that Lefebvre des Noëttes could find only two pictorial representations from the tenth century. Had he not found even these, would he have dated the invention from the eleventh century? Cf. Bloch, "Les 'Inventions' médiévales," *loc. cit.*, p. 640, n. 2. For further views as to the date of the horse collar, tandem harness, and so on in Europe, see E. M. Jope, "Vehicles and Harness," in *A History of Technology*, II (Oxford, 1956), 538, 554 f., and R. J. Forbes, "Power," *ibid.*, pp. 592 f. The views presented in this work naturally may vary widely, e.g., the two cited here.

75. Bloch, "The Rise of Dependent Cultivation," CEH, I, 226.

76. Haudricourt, "De l'Origine de l'attelage," *loc. cit.*, pp. 521–22. Forbes, "Power," *loc. cit.*, p. 592, would place its introduction into Europe in the early Middle Ages.

77. Bloch, *Les Caractères*, pp. 51–53; Bloch, "Champs et villages," *Annales*,

VI, 474 ff.; Parain, "The Evolution of Agricultural Technique," CEH, I, 139; Reginald Lennard, "From Roman Britain to Anglo-Saxon England," *Wirtschaft und Kultur* (the Dopsch Festschrift), pp. 69–70; R. G. Collingwood, "Roman Britain," in *An Economic Survey of Ancient Rome*, III, 77–78. See also Jope, "Agricultural Implements," in *A History of Technology*, II, 86–91.

78. Bloch, *Les Caractères*, pp. 53–54, and White, "Technology and Invention," *loc. cit.*, p. 151. The *araire* could, of course, be used elsewhere, on light or soft soil, and because of its relative cheapness was widely used on small holdings. See Parain, "Agricultural Technique," *loc. cit.*, p. 140.

79. *Ibid.*

80. White, *loc. cit.*, 151, and on the last point Bloch, *Les Caractères*, pp. 56–57. Note also the general remarks of A. C. Crombie, *Augustine to Galileo: The History of Science A.D. 400–1650* (London, 1952), p. 159. Crombie makes no effort to trace the origin of the wheeled plow equipped with coulter, horizontal share, and mouldboard beyond referring to it as "the heavy Saxon wheeled plough."

81. White, *loc. cit.*, pp. 151–52. Parain, who calls it "the great agricultural novelty of the Middle Ages" (*loc. cit.*, p. 127), also believes it could not go back much beyond the Carolingian period. Bloch, *Les Caractères*, p. 34, suggests a date even earlier than the later eighth century. Cf. Dauvergne, "Supplément," p. 36.

82. Parain, *loc. cit.*, pp. 128–29. See Bloch, *Les Caractères*, pp. 31 ff., for some of the problems and puzzles involved in determining where the biennial and where the triennial system of rotation of crops and fallow was established. Cf. Grand, *L'Agriculture*, pp. 270–71. The questions raised by Bloch, especially on pp. 34–35, invite further consideration. Why was the three-field system not introduced into regions of France from which climatic and geographical conditions did not bar it and where it would have increased production as it did elsewhere? Could this be an example of ingrained devotion to age-old methods, of stout resistance to change? An affirmative reply would raise still more questions. Obviously no simple answer will do. See also Bloch, "Champs et villages," *loc. cit.*, p. 479, and "Les 'Inventions' médiévales," *loc. cit.*, pp. 637–38. The distribution of the two systems has long been a puzzle; cf. N. S. B. Gras, *A History of Agriculture in Europe and America* (New York, 1925), pp. 29 f.

83. Parain, *loc. cit.*, p. 128. See also the report on the session "New Light on a Dark Age: A Symposium of Western Civilization in the Tenth Century," presented at the sixty-seventh annual meeting of the American Historical Association, December 28, 29, and 30, 1952, in Washington, D.C., and published in the *American Historical Review*, LVIII (1953), 744–45, particularly the summaries of the remarks made by Robert S. Lopez and Lynn White. These papers were subsequently published in *Medievalia et Humanistica*, as indicated in Chapter II above. Note also Bloch, *Les Caractères*, p. 34.

84. Grand, *L'Agriculture,* pp. 275–76; Parain, *loc. cit.,* pp. 133–34. Parain notes that the friends of the ox could have added that he is less liable to disease and his harness is cheaper.

85. See White's statement, "Technology and Invention," *loc. cit.,* pp. 154–55. For one much less positive, cf. Parain, *loc. cit.,* pp. 129–30.

86. White, *loc. cit.,* p. 154. For the distribution according to size of holdings, see Parain, *loc. cit.,* p. 130.

87. Bloch, "Avènement et conquêtes du moulin à eau," *Annales,* VII, 538, 544–45. It is a commonplace that the Romans were practical, if in a somewhat narrow-minded way, and that at least they excelled in the military and engineering techniques which aimed at conquest and administration. There is much truth in this assumption, but it is all the more notable that recent research has considerably modified their prestige as road builders. See Lefebvre des Noëttes, *L'Attelage,* pp. 165–73; White, *loc. cit.,* pp. 150–51; Lot, FMA, p. 518. On the water mill see also Dauvergne, "Supplément," pp. 141 ff.

88. "Moulin à eau," *loc. cit.,* pp. 545–48.

89. *Ibid.,* p. 547.

90. *Ibid.,* pp. 548 ff. It is not surprising to find evidence of stout resistance to seigniorial authority in the matter of using the lord's mill, even though it was more efficient than the old methods (see *ibid.,* pp. 552–53). Certainly this meant a kind of refusal to profit by technical progress; but other things were involved, viz., opposition to authority and monopoly, a strong desire for the greatest possible independence on the part of the peasants, and sometimes no doubt the expense involved in using the lord's superior mill. Note, for example, that C. L. Sagui, "La Meunerie de Barbegal (France) et les roues hydrauliques chez les anciens et au moyen âge," *Isis,* XXXVIII (1948), 229, speculates that the mill at Barbegal might have been built in the third or fourth century "in an economic atmosphere of catastrophe." Note his other comments on the economic condition of the Later Empire and industrial machinery (pp. 227, 231).

91. *Ibid.,* pp. 553–54. Lefebvre des Noëttes, *L'Attelage,* p. 121, and "La 'Nuit' du moyen âge et son inventaire," *Mercure de France,* CCXXXV (1932), 575–76, would connect the increased use of the water mill, which he attributed incorrectly to the twelfth century, with the new system of harnessing.

92. White, "Technology and Invention," *loc. cit.,* p. 153; Crombie, *Augustine to Galileo,* p. 166.

93. *L'Attelage,* especially pp. 184–88. The subtitle of this work, it will be remembered, is *Contribution à l'histoire de l'esclavage.* Cf. Bloch, "Les 'Inventions' médiévales," *loc. cit.,* pp. 640–43, and see the interesting observations of Friedrich Oertel, "The Economic Life of the Empire," *Cambridge Ancient History,* XII (1939), 232–81, especially pp. 252 ff. on technology and the Roman economy, and on the same subject Frank W. Walbank, *The Decline of the Roman Empire in the West* (London, 1946), pp. 66–75. Walbank perhaps

simplifies a little too much the relationship between "low techniques" and slavery as an explanation of the Roman economic failure. His discussion here (pp. 66–75) and in the following pages is extremely provocative.

94. "Technique et évolution sociale," *loc. cit.*, pp. 96 ff. On the meanings of *servus* see also Verlinden, *L'Esclavage*, I, 739 ff.

95. It seems to me regrettable that Crombie does not refer to Bloch's arguments against Lefebvre des Noëttes' views in respect of slavery but simply concludes (*Augustine to Galileo*, p. 165): "The new methods of harnessing animal power, and the increasing exploitation of water- and wind-power, came to make slavery unnecessary." Note the rather odd views of Bertrand Gille, "Machines," in *A History of Technology*, II, 638–39. Gille also makes no reference to Bloch's answer to Lefebvre des Noëttes, though he does refer indirectly to the latter, e.g., "The argument attributing the disappearance of slavery to the change from the yoke to the horse-collar . . . is also unconvincing."

96. Arnold J. Toynbee, *A Study of History*, I, 39, 332 (pp. 10 and 78 in the abridged edition). No doubt I belabor the point, but I must record again my objection to the "Dark Age" concept of the early medieval period. A fallacy for which Gibbon may be pardoned because of the strong and blinding biases of his age cannot be permitted to go unchallenged today. The erroneous assumptions which gave rise to the designation have been almost universally repudiated by specialists; yet the misleading term persists. Examples are many; I shall cite only two in addition to those already mentioned. Charles Singer in *A Short History of Science* (Oxford, 1941) adds to his fifth chapter, "The Failure of Knowledge," the subtitle "The Middle Ages (About A.D. 400–1400): Theology, Queen of the Sciences." The first section of this chapter, "The Dark Age (400–1000)," very briefly refers to such figures as Boethius, Isidore, and Gerbert, wholly omitting the technological advances of the period. It is also announced (p. 126) that the medieval millennium "is divided unequally by an event of the highest importance for the human intellect," i.e., the "remarkable development of intellectual activity in Islam" from ca. 900 to 1200. A. C. Crombie in the *Augustine to Galileo* also retains the concept of the Dark Ages, during which "natural knowledge continued to be considered of very secondary importance" (p. 7). "In Western Christendom in the Dark Ages men were concerned more to preserve the facts which had been collected in classical times than to attempt original interpretations themselves." Crombie corrects to some extent the misleading impression given by this sentence when he goes on at once to say, "Yet, during this period, a new element was added from the social situation, an activist attitude which initiated a period of technical invention and was to have an important effect on the development of scientific apparatus" (pp. xiv–xv). Lynn Thorndike, in reviewing this work, (*Speculum*, XXIX (1954), 541–45), calls attention to Crombie's retention of the term "Dark Ages," and to his numerous references to the Arabs "without once explaining that he really means writers in Arabic, who

might be Persians, Syrians, Egyptians, Moors, Spaniards, Jews, or Christians" (pp. 541–42). As a counterweight to these perhaps excessive appreciations of the "Arab" contribution, note the thought-provoking comments of Ferdinand Lot, *Les Invasions barbares et le peuplement de l'Europe. Introduction à l'intel ligence des derniers traités de paix* (Paris, 1937), particularly in the "Conclusion de la première partie," pp. 109–14. Surely historians of science above all others might be expected to avoid blanket denunciations and outworn generalities. Perhaps no other group of historians has had so good an opportunity to find that all ages are at least to some extent dark, that superstition still exists, and that even their own times might conceivably be described as suffering from a "failure of knowledge."

97. *L'Attelage,* p. 188.

98. Toynbee, *A Study of History,* e.g., I, 61 (p. 14 in the abridged edition).

99. Bloch, "Note sur un grand problème d'influences," *Annales,* VIII, 513 f.

100. Lefebvre des Nöettes, *L'Attelage,* pp. 238–46, and Grand, *L'Agriculture,* pp. 450–51. Lot, *L'Art militaire et les armées au moyen âge en Europe et dans le Proche Orient* (Paris, 1946), I, 19–20, would date the ascendancy of cavalry to the fourth century or even the third.

101. Grand, *L'Agriculture,* pp. 451–52.

102. *L'Attelage,* p. 235.

103. *Ibid.,* p. 236. I have not been able to consult the work of Claudio Sánchez-Albornoz y Menduina, *En torno a los orígines del feudalismo* (Mendoza, 1942), which is discussed by Grand, *L'Agriculture,* pp. 449–50. See also the remarks of R. S. Lopez in his review in *Speculum,* XXIV (1949), 287–88. If Sánchez-Albornoz is correct in believing that the Arabs were scarcely better supplied with horses than the Franks at the time of Poitiers, Brunner's well-known thesis would indeed be shaken. Note also that, in Lopez's words, "Senor Sánchez not only denies that Charles Martel was forced to seize land of the Church in order to create a cavalry of vassals, but he also doubts that the union of vassalship and *beneficium* created feudalism all of a sudden under Charles Martel and his immediate successors." One thing at least is clear: the political and social developments leading to feudalism were well on their way before the rise of heavy cavalry. The remark that it was not the Arabs or Franks who had a large cavalry in the eighth century but the Lombards, the Aquitanians, the Basques, and later the Magyars is very interesting. Cf. Carl Stephenson's discussion of great horses in "Feudalism and Its Antecedents in England," *American Historical Review,* XLVIII (1943), 259–60.

104. Sagui, "La Meunerie de Barbegal," *loc. cit.,* pp. 229–31.

105. Rostovtzeff, *Social and Economic History of the Roman Empire,* p. 166.

106. It is true also, of course, that some ancient methods, e.g. marling, were less used than before. In the case of marling this was apparently because of the

expense. See Parain, "The Evolution of Agricultural Technique," CEH, I, 135–36. No doubt sometimes useful techniques were simply lost or given up for no good reason at all, but in general it is safe to say that medieval agriculturalists lost very little and added a great deal.

107. See, for example, Curtis Wilson, *William Heytesbury. Medieval Logic and the Rise of Mathematical Physics* (Madison, Wis., 1956), and the review of it by Andrew G. O'Connor, *Speculum,* XXXII (1957), 622–24.

NOTES TO CHAPTER V

1. Geoffrey Barraclough (*History in a Changing World,* p. 41) would not go nearly so far, though he acknowledges that "in the hands of St. Ambrose, St. Leo and St. Augustine western Christianity took shape as something different from the orthodox faith of the east." He contends against the view that this "difference" consisted in the assimilation or adoption of Roman culture by the West, and he rightly rejects the opinion (whose, he does not say) that this "difference" alone marked a decisive break.

2. Barraclough (*ibid.*) has noted that East and West both inherited from the classical past, but he is interested in demonstrating the "universal content" of civilization and deplores any attempt to distinguish between the Eastern and Western traditions or to see any contrast between them. His attempts to make one big happy family of the contemporary world apparently derive from his feeling that historically the day of Europe and European civilization is over. This judgment seems to me premature. Are we to conclude that the wish is mother to the thought? The Orient is struggling today to throw off not only foreign domination but home-grown slave and caste systems, "religious" superstitions, and the virtual serfdom of the masses. Its leaders are receptive to Western ideas and experiments in democracy and education, and even to the Western technology which Toynbee and some others find so objectionable. Barraclough is wrong in assuming that the West and the Western tradition are hostile to the East. Admittedly, Western imperialists have exploited the East, but they have done the same, when they could, to their own people. As individuals they rank no better in the Western tradition than Brahmans and nabobs of all varieties in the Oriental. Both civilizations have much, in their respective pasts, to win free of. The East's worst enemy is not the West but its own past; it is this tyranny, more than any other, that it is now trying to throw off. See Butterfield's comment on this view of Barraclough's in his review of *History in a Changing World, loc. cit.,* p. 190. See also Pieter Geyl's review, *The Nation,* CLXXXIV (1957), 325–27.

3. See the recent searching study of concepts of liberty in the Middle Ages by Herbert Grundmann, "Freiheit als religiöses, politisches und persönliches Postulat im Mittelalter," *Historische Zeitschrift,* CLXXXIII (1957), 23–53. As noted with reference to the researches of Bloch and Verlinden, the meaning of such

words as *liber* and *servus* underwent changes with reference to both earlier and later definitions and also within the medieval period. The semantic problem involved is one often encountered today, as anyone who has tried to define the meanings of "liberal" since the Enlightenment knows.

4. For a recent discussion of this subject and historicism, see Barraclough, *History in a Changing World,* pp. 2–7, 11–12, and the references there given. Naturally enough the definitions of historicism vary somewhat. Barraclough, perhaps as a recent convert, is a little overzealous and inclined to have recourse a trifle too hastily to the boot and thumbscrew. One wonders also if Karl Popper, who is cited by Barraclough, is not himself sometimes the victim of ideas as fixed as those of the social scientists he attacks, always with vigor and often with effect. A good example is his treatment of Plato, who has now been slowly burning at the stake for some years. It may not be out of place to inquire whether the Grand Inquisitors are sometimes elected by the democratic processes of an open society or whether they always appoint themselves. I ask of course only as one Inquisitor, admittedly self-appointed, to another.

Perhaps an even better illustration of the fact that Popper too can look at history with blinders—the "historicistic" are not the only variety—is his treatment of the Middle Ages. Much of what he says about the "dark ages" is plain nonsense, the product of ignorance, reliance upon interpretations and clichés long rejected, and prejudice. Good motives, such as devotion to liberty and antipathy for political despotism, do not wholly atone for breaches of so serious a nature. Popper knows this, however, for he quotes Acton on the subject. A further illustration of his bias, or perhaps only of the sparseness of his information on some subjects, is his refutation of the Romantic fallacies and illusions about the Middle Ages without a word on the Rationalist fancies at the other extreme. As I have remarked before, *both errors* were the result of special pleading applied to history, and it may be added that one is as "historicistic" as the other. Popper rather clearly indicates his feeling that some brands of historicism are not so bad as others—Marx, for example, being somewhat less repulsive to him as a rationalist than certain other thinkers with whom he disagrees. See K. R. Popper, *The Open Society and Its Enemies,* 2d ed. (London, 1952), I, 1–5, for his first definitions of historicism; for his views on the "allegedly 'Christian' authoritarianism of the Middle Ages," II, 23–26, 302–3; for the citation of Acton, II, 303; for reference to the Romantic eulogistic view of the Middle Ages, II, 302–3; and for the basis of my remark about Popper on Marx, II, 252 ff.

In thus criticizing Popper's relative gentleness with Marx, I by no means wish to imply approval of the views and methods of Arnold J. Toynbee, who is also discussed here by Popper. My objection is that there seems to be more lenience for Marx than for, say, A. N. Whitehead (for whom see Popper, II, 247 ff.). Whitehead is presented to us, perhaps a trifle smugly, as an irrationalist, though an unwitting one.

5. "Les 'Inventions' médiévales," *Annales,* VII, 639.

6. "Moulin à eau," *Annales,* VII, 545–48.

7. As noted above, Barraclough (*History in a Changing World,* p. 41), to mention only one, would not agree.

8. In three remarkable essays, "The History of Freedom in Antiquity" and "The History of Freedom in Christianity," both published in 1877, and "Sir Erskine May's Democracy in Europe," published in 1878. See *The History of Freedom and Other Essays,* edited by J. N. Figgis and R. B. Laurence (London, 1909), pp. 1–29, 30–60, 61–100. For more specific reference to the ideas of this and the following sentences, pp. 25–29, 34–39, 79–85.

9. *Ibid.,* p. 29.

10. *Ibid.,* p. 60.

11. *The Idea of History* (Oxford, 1946), p. 333.

Bibliography

LIST OF ABBREVIATIONS

CAH: *Cambridge Ancient History*
CEH: *Cambridge Economic History*
CMH: *Cambridge Medieval History*
CSEL: *Corpus Scriptorum Ecclesiasticorum Latinorum*
EHR: *Economic History Review*
SSCI: *Settimane di studio del centro italiano di studi sull'alto medioevo*

Acton, John Emerich Edward Dalberg, First Baron Acton. The History of Freedom and Other Essays. Edited by J. N. Figgis and Reginald V. Laurence. London, 1909.

Adams, George Burton. "The Present Problems of Medieval History," in Vol. III of International Congress of Arts and Science. London and New York, 1906.

Andréadès, André M. "Public Finances: Currency, Public Expenditure, Budget, Public Revenue," in Byzantium, edited by Norman H. Baynes and H. St.L. B. Moss. Oxford, 1948.

Aubin, Hermann. "Die Frage nach der Scheide zwischen Altertum und Mittelalter," *Historische Zeitschrift*, CLXXII (1951), 245–63.

Bark, William C. "Theodoric vs. Boethius: Vindication and Apology," *American Historical Review*, XLIX (1944), 410–26.

Barraclough, Geoffrey. History in a Changing World. Oxford, 1955.

Baynes, Norman H. "The Decline of the Roman Power in Western Europe. Some Modern Explanations," *Journal of Roman Studies*, XXXIII (1943), 29–35.

———. Review of Ferdinand Lot, La Fin du monde antique et le début du moyen âge (Paris, 1927); Henri Pirenne, Les Villes du moyen âge, Essai d'histoire économique et sociale (Brussels, 1927); and Michael Rostovtzeff, The Social and Economic History of the Roman Empire (Oxford, 1926) in *Journal of Roman Studies*, XIX (1929), 224–35.

Bertolini, Ottorino. " 'Gothia' e 'Romania,' " SSCI, III (1956), 13–33.

Blake, Robert P. "The Monetary Reform of Anastasius I and Its Economic Implications," in Studies in the History of Culture. Menasha, Wis., 1942.

Bloch, Marc. "Avènement et conquêtes du moulin à eau," *Annales d'histoire économique et sociale*, VII (1935), 538–63.

———. Les Caractères originaux de l'histoire rurale française. New ed. Paris, 1952.

———. "Champs et villages," *Annales d'histoire économique et sociale*, VI (1934), 467–89.

———. "Les 'Inventions' médiévales," *Annales d'histoire économique et sociale,* VII (1935), 634–43.

———. "Le Problème de l'or au moyen âge," *Annales d'histoire économique et sociale,* V (1933), 1–34.

———. Review of Rudolf Buchner, Die Provence in merowingischer Zeit. Verfassung-Wirtschaft-Kultur (Stuttgart, 1933), in *Annales d'histoire économique et sociale,* VI (1934), 188–89.

———. "The Rise of Dependent Cultivation and Seigniorial Institutions," CEH, I (1941), 224–77.

———. "Technique et évolution sociale. A propos de l'histoire de l'attelage et de celle de l'esclavage," *Revue de synthèse historique,* XLI (1926), 91–99.

———. "Les Techniques, l'histoire et la vie. Note sur un grand problème d'influences," *Annales d'histoire économique et sociale,* VIII (1936), 513–15.

Boethius, Anicius Manlius Severinus. Philosophiae consolatio. Edited by Edward K. Rand and Hugh F. Stewart. New York, 1918.

Boissonade, Prosper. Life and Work in Medieval Europe (Fifth to Fifteenth Centuries). Translated by Eileen Power. New York, 1927.

Bolin, Sture. "Mohammed, Charlemagne and Ruric," *The Scandinavian Economic History Review,* I (1953), 5–39.

Boyce, Gray Cowan. "The Legacy of Henri Pirenne," *Byzantion,* XV (1940–41), 449–64.

Bratianu, G. I. "La Distribution de l'or et les raisons économiques de la division de l'Empire romain," *Études byzantines d'histoire économique et sociale.* Paris, 1938.

———. "Une Nouvelle Histoire de l'Europe au moyen âge: La fin du monde antique et le triomphe de l'Orient," *Revue belge de philologie et d'histoire,* XVIII (1939), 252–66.

Bréhier, Louis, and René Aigrain. Grégoire le grand, les états barbares et la conquête arabe (590–757). Vol. V. of Histoire de l'Église depuis les origines jusqu'à nos jours. Edited by Augustin Fliche and Victor Martin. Paris, 1947.

Broglie, Albert de. L'Église et l'Empire romain au IVe siècle. 2d ed. Vol. II. Paris, 1857.

Brutzkus, J. "Trade with Eastern Europe, 800–1200," EHR, XIII (1943), 31–41.

Burckhardt, Jakob. Weltgeschichtliche Betrachtungen. Berlin and Stuttgart, 1910.

Bury, J. B. A History of the Later Roman Empire from Arcadius to Irene (395 A.D. to 800 A.D.). Vol. I. London, 1889.

———. History of the Later Roman Empire from the Death of Theodosius I to the Death of Justinian (A.D. 395 to A.D. 565). Vol. II. London, 1923.

Butterfield, Herbert. Man on His Past. The Study of the History of Historical Scholarship. Cambridge, England, 1955.

———. Review of Geoffrey Barraclough, History in a Changing World (Oxford, 1955), in *The Cambridge Historical Journal,* XII (1956), 189–91.

Calmette, Joseph. Charlemagne. Sa vie et son oeuvre. Paris, 1945.

———. Le Monde féodal. Paris, 1946.

Cecchelli, Carlo. "Motivi orientali e occidentali nell'arte del periodo dei Goti in Italia," SSCI, III (1956), 43–55 and Tav. I–V.

Cipolla, Carlo M. "Encore Mahomet et Charlemagne. L'Économie politique au secours de l'histoire. Sur un façon de comprendre l'histoire qui est nôtre," *Annales,* IV (1949), 4–9.

Cochrane, Charles N. Christianity and Classical Culture. A Study of Thought and Action from Augustus to Augustine. Toronto, 1944.

Collingwood, R. G. The Idea of History. Oxford, 1946.

———. "Roman Britain," in Vol. III of An Economic Survey of Ancient Rome, edited by Tenney Frank. Baltimore, 1937.

Coulton, G. G. The Medieval Scene. New York, 1931.

Courcelle, Pierre. Histoire littéraire des grandes invasions germaniques. Paris, 1948.

Crombie, A. C. Augustine to Galileo: The History of Science A.D. 400–1650. London, 1952.

Curtius, Ernst R. Europäische Literatur und lateinisches Mittelalter. Bern, 1948.

Dauvergne, Robert. Supplément établi d'après les travaux de l'auteur (1931–1944). Vol. II of Marc Bloch, Les Caractères originaux de l'histoire rurale française. Paris, 1956.

Davis, Elmer. "Are We Worth Saving? And If So, Why?" in But We Were Born Free. Indianapolis and New York, 1953.

Dawson, Christopher. The Making of Europe: An Introduction to the History of European Unity. London, 1948.

Deanesly, Margaret. A History of Early Medieval Europe, 476–911. London, 1956.

Demougeot, Émilienne. De l'Unité à la division de l'Empire romain, 395–410: Essai sur le gouvernement impérial. Paris, 1951.

Dennett, Daniel C., Jr. "Pirenne and Muhammad," *Speculum,* XXIII (1948), 165–90.

Dill, Sir Samuel. Roman Society in the Last Century of the Western Empire. 2d ed., revised. London, 1905.

Dopsch, Alfons. "Agrarian Institutions of the Germanic Kingdoms from the Fifth to the Ninth Century," CEH, I (1941), 169–93.

———. "Vom Altertum zum Mittelalter: Das Kontinuitäts-problem," *Archiv für Kulturgeschichte,* XVI (1926), 159–82.

———. "Naturalwirtschaft und Geldwirtschaft in der Weltgeschichte," in Beiträge zur Sozial- und Wirtschaftsgeschichte. Vienna, 1938.

———. Festschrift Dopsch—Wirtschaft und Kultur: Festschrift zum 70. Geburtstag von Alfons Dopsch. Baden bei Wien, 1938.

Duchesne, Louis. Histoire ancienne de l'église. 2d ed. Vol. III. Paris, 1910.

Duckett, Eleanor S. Anglo-Saxon Saints and Scholars. New York, 1947.

Ensslin, Wilhelm. "The Emperor and the Imperial Administration," in Byzantium, edited by N. H. Baynes and H. St.L. B. Moss. Oxford, 1948.

Espinas, Georges. "Les Origines du patriciat urbain. Henri Pirenne s'est-il trompé? II: La discussion," *Annales,* I (1946), 148–53.

Febvre, Lucien. "Fils de riches ou nouveaux riches," *Annales,* I (1946), 139–42.

Focillon, Henri. L'An mil. Paris, 1952.

———. Moyen Age: Survivances et réveils. Études d'art et d'histoire. Montreal, 1945.

Folz, Robert. L'Idée d'Empire en Occident du Ve au XIVe siècle. Paris, 1953.

Forbes, R. J. "Power," in Vol. II of A History of Technology. Oxford, 1956.

Fustel de Coulanges. Les Origines du système féodal. Le bénéfice et le patronat pendant l'époque mérovingienne. Paris, 1890.

———. Les Transformations de la royauté pendant l'époque carolingienne. Paris, 1892.

Ganshof, François L. Feudalism. Translated by Philip Grierson. 1st English edition, based on the 2d French edition but having numerous corrections and additions. London, 1952.

———. "Medieval Agrarian Society in Its Prime. Section I. France, the Low Countries, and Western Germany," CEH, I (1941), 278–322.

———. "Note sur les ports de Provence du VIIIe au Xe siècle," *Revue historique,* CLXXXIII (1938), 28–37.

———. "L'Origine des rapports féodo-vassaliques: Les rapports féodo-vassaliques dans la monarchie franque au Nord des Alpes à l'époque carolingienne," SSCI, I (1954), 27–69.

Geffcken, Johannes. "Stimmungen im untergehenden Weströmerreich," *Neue Jahrbücher für das klassische Altertum, Geschichte und deutsche Literatur,* XXIII (1920), 256–69.

Gibbon, Edward. The History of the Decline and Fall of the Roman Empire. 5th ed., edited by J. B. Bury. Vol. V. London, 1923.

Gille, Bertrand. "Machines," in Vol. II of A History of Technology. Oxford, 1956.

Grand, Roger. L'Agriculture au moyen âge de la fin de l'Empire romain au XVIe siècle. Paris, 1950.

———. "Les Moyens de résoudre dans le haut moyen âge les problèmes ruraux," SSCI, II (1955), 523–46.

Gras, N. S. B. A History of Agriculture in Europe and America. New York, 1925.

Greenaway, George W. Saint Boniface. Three Biographical Studies for the Twelfth Centenary Festival. London, 1955.

Grégoire, Henri. "The Byzantine Church," in Byzantium, edited by N. H. Baynes and H. St.L. B. Moss. Oxford, 1948.

Gregory of Tours. Opera. Pars I. Historia Francorum. In MGH, Scriptores rerum Merovingicarum, I. Hannover, 1884.

Grenier, Albert. "La Gaule romaine," in Vol. III of An Economic Survey of Ancient Rome, edited by Tenney Frank. Baltimore, 1937.

Grundmann, Herbert. "Freiheit als religiöses, politisches und persönliches Postulat im Mittelalter," *Historische Zeitschrift,* CLXXXIII (1957), 23–53.

Gwatkin, H. M. "Constantine and His City," CMH, I (2d ed., 1924), 1–23.

———, and J. P. Whitney, "Preface to Volume I," CMH, I (2d ed., 1924), vii–ix.

Halecki, Oscar. "Projets d'articles sur les mots Divisions et Moyen Age," in "Bulletin du Centre international de synthèse, Section de synthèse historique," No. 2 (December, 1926), pp. 16–22. Appended to *Revue de synthèse historique,* XLII (1926).

Hardy, Edward R. The Large Estates of Byzantine Egypt. New York, 1931.

Hartmann, Ludo M. Ein Kapitel vom spätantiken und frühmittelalterlichen Staate. Berlin, 1913.

Haudricourt, André-G. "De l'Origine de l'attelage moderne," *Annales,* VIII (1936), 515–22.

Hofbauer, Silvester. Die Ausbildung der grossen Grandherrschaften im Reiche der Merowinger. Vienna, 1927.

Hubert, Jean. "Quelques Sources de l'art carolingien: Résumé," SSCI, I (1954), 215–19.

Jerome. Commentariorum in Ezechielem prophetam libri quatuordecim. In J. P. Migne, Patrologiae cursus completus; series latina, XXV. Paris, 1884.

———. Epistulae, Pars III: Epistulae CXXI–CLIV. Edited by J. Hilberg. In Vol. LVI of CSEL. Vienna, 1918.

Johnson, Allan C., and Louis C. West. Byzantine Egypt: Economic Studies. Princeton, 1949.

Jope, E. M. "Agricultural Implements," in Vol. II of A History of Technology. Oxford, 1956.

———. "Vehicles and Harness," in Vol. II of A History of Technology. Oxford, 1956.

Joranson, Einar. Review of Pirenne, Mahomet et Charlemagne, in *American Historical Review,* XLIV (1938–39), 324–25.

Kaphan, Fritz. Zwischen Antike und Mittelalter. Das Donau-Alpenland im Zeitalter St. Severins. Munich, ca. 1946.

Katz, Solomon. The Jews in the Visigothic and Frankish Kingdoms of Spain and Gaul. Cambridge, Mass., 1937.

Koebner, Richard. "The Settlement and Colonisation of Europe," CEH, I (1941), 1–88.

Kroell, Maurice. L'Immunité franque. Paris, 1910.

Labriolle, Pierre de. Histoire de la littérature latine chrétienne. 3d ed., revised by Gustave Bardy. Paris, 1947.

Laistner, M. L. W. Christianity and Pagan Culture in the Later Roman Empire together with an English Translation of John Chrysostom's Address on

Vainglory and the Right Way for Parents to Bring Up Their Children. Ithaca, N.Y., 1951.

————. "Pagan Schools and Christian Teachers," in Liber Floridus: Mittellateinische Studien. Festschrift Paul Lehmann, edited by Bernhard Bischoff and Suso Brechter. Erzabtei St. Ottilien, 1950.

————. Thought and Letters in Western Europe, A.D. 500 to 900. 2d ed. Ithaca, N.Y., 1957.

Latouche, Robert. Les Grandes Invasions et la crise de l'Occident au Ve siècle. Paris, 1946.

————. Les Origines de l'économie occidentale. Paris, 1956.

Lefebvre des Noëttes. L'Attelage et le cheval de selle à travers les âges. Contribution à l'histoire de l'esclavage. Paris, 1931.

————. "La Force motrice animale et le rôle des inventions techniques," *Revue de synthèse historique*, XLIII (1927), 83–91.

————. De la Marine antique à la marine moderne. La révolution du gouvernail. Contribution à l'étude de l'esclavage. Paris, 1935.

————. "La 'Nuit' du moyen âge et son inventaire," *Mercure de France*, CCXXXV (1932), 572–99.

Lehmann, Paul. "Das Problem der karolingischen Renaissance," SSCI, I (1954), 309–57.

Leicht, Pier Silverio. "Il Feudo in Italia nell'età carolingia," SSCI, I (1954), 71–107.

Lennard, Reginald. "From Roman Britain to Anglo-Saxon England," in Festschrift Dopsch. Baden bei Wien, 1938.

Lestocquoy, Abbé Jean. "Les Origines du patriciat urbain. Henri Pirenne s'est-il trompé? I: La thèse," *Annales*, I (1946), 143–48.

————. "De l'Unité à la pluralité: Le paysage urbain en Gaule du Ve au VIe siècle," *Annales*, VIII (1953), 159–72.

Lewis, Archibald R. "Le Commerce et la navigation sur les côtes atlantiques de la Gaule du Ve au VIIIe siècle," *Le Moyen Age*, LIX (1953), 247–98.

————. Naval Power and Trade in the Mediterranean, A.D. 500–1100. Princeton, 1951.

Lietzmann, Hans. "Das Problem der Spätantike," in Sitzungsberichte der preussischen Akademie der Wissenschaften, Philosophisch-historische Klasse, XXXI (1927), 342–58.

Löfstedt, Einar. Coniectanea: Untersuchungen auf dem Gebiete der antiken und mittelalterlichen Latinität. Uppsala and Stockholm, 1950.

Lombard, Maurice. "Les Bases monétaires d'une suprématie économique. L'Or musulman du VIIIe au XIe siècle," *Annales*, II (1947), 143–60.

————. "Mahomet et Charlemagne. Le Problème économique," *Annales*, III (1948), 188–99.

Lopez, Robert S. "Du Marché temporaire à la colonie permanente. L'évolution de la politique commerciale au moyen âge," *Annales*, IV (1949), 389–405.

———. "Mohammed and Charlemagne: A Revision," *Speculum,* XVIII (1943), 14–38.

———. Review of Claudio Sánchez-Albornoz y Menduina, En torno a los orígines del feudalismo (Mendoza, 1942), in *Speculum,* XXIV (1949), 285–89.

Lot, Ferdinand. L'Art militaire et les armées au moyen âge en Europe et dans le Proche Orient. 2 vols. Paris, 1946.

———. La Fin du monde antique et le début du moyen âge. 2d ed. Paris, 1951.

———. La Gaule. Les fondements ethniques, sociaux et politiques de la nation française. Paris, 1947.

———. "Un Grand Domaine à l'époque franque. Ardin en Poitou, Contribution à l'étude de l'impôt." Fasc. 230 of Bibliothèque de l'École des Hautes Études. Paris, 1921.

———. L'Impôt foncier et la capitation personnelle sous le Bas-Empire et à l'époque franque. Paris, 1928.

———. Les Invasions barbares et le peuplement de l'Europe. Introduction à l'intelligence des derniers traités de paix. Paris, 1937.

———. Les Invasions germaniques. La pénétration mutuelle du monde barbare et du monde romain. Paris, 1945.

———. Nouvelles Recherches sur l'impôt foncier et la capitation personnelle sous le Bas-Empire. Fasc. 304 of Bibliothèque de l'École des Hautes Études. Paris, 1955.

———. Recherches sur la population et la superficie des cités remontant à la période gallo-romaine. Paris, 1945–47 and 1950.

———, and François L. Ganshof. Les Destinées de l'Empire en Occident de 395 à 888. Vol. I, Part 2: "De 768 à 888." Paris, 1941.

Loyen, André. Recherches historiques sur les panégyriques de Sidoine Apollinaire. Fasc. 285 of Bibliothèque de l'École des Hautes Études. Paris, 1942.

———. Sidoine Apollinaire et l'esprit précieux en Gaule aux derniers jours de l'Empire. Paris, 1943.

Luzzatto, Gino. "Mutamenti nell'economia agraria italiana dalla caduta dei Carolingi al principio del sec. XI," SSCI, II (1955), 601–22.

———. Storia economica d'Italia. Vol. I. Rome, 1949.

McIlwain, C. H. "The Historian's Part in a Changing World," *American Historical Review,* XLII (1937), 207–24.

Mâle, Émile. La Fin du paganisme en Gaule et les plus anciennes basiliques chrétiennes. Paris, 1950.

Marrou, Henri-Irénée. Histoire de l'éducation dans l'antiquité. Paris, 1948.

———. Saint-Augustin et la fin de la culture antique. Paris, 1938.

Mickwitz, Gunnar. Geld und Wirtschaft im römischen Reich des vierten Jahrhunderts n. Chr. Vol. IV, No. 2, publications of the Societas Scientiarum Fennica, Commentationes Humanarum Litterarum. Helsingfors, 1932.

————. "Le Problème de l'or dans le monde antique," *Annales d'histoire écono-mique et sociale,* VI (1934), 235–47.

————. "Der Verkehr auf dem westlichen Mittelmeer um 600 n. Chr.," in Festschrift Dopsch. Baden bei Wien, 1938.

Momigliano, Arnaldo. Review of (1) Pirenne, Mohammed and Charlemagne, and (2) Robert S. Lopez, "Mohammed and Charlemagne: A Revision" [*Speculum,* XVIII (1943), 14–38], in *Journal of Roman Studies,* XXXIV (1944), 157–58.

Mommsen, Theodor. "St. Augustine and the Christian Idea of Progress," *Journal of the History of Ideas,* XII (1951), 346–74.

Monteverdi, Angelo. "Il problema del rinascimento carolino," SSCI, I (1954), 359–72.

Morey, Charles R. Mediaeval Art. New York, 1942.

Moss, H. St.L. B. "The Economic Consequences of the Barbarian Invasions," EHR, VII (1936–37), 209–16.

Oertel, Friedrich. "The Economic Life of the Empire," CAH, XII (1939), 232–81.

Ohnsorge, Werner. Das Zweikaiserproblem im früheren Mittelalter: Die Be-deutung des byzantinischen Reiches für die Entwicklung der Staatsidee in Europa. Hildesheim, 1947.

Orosius, Paulus. Historiarum adversum paganos libri vii. Edited by Karl F. W. Zangemeister. Vol. VII of CSEL. Vienna, 1882.

Ostrogorsky, Georg. "Agrarian Conditions in the Byzantine Empire in the Middle Ages," CEH, I (1941), 194–223.

Palol de Salellas, Pedro. "Esencia del arte hispánico de época visigoda: Roma-nismo y germanismo," SSCI, III (1956), 65–126 and Tav. I–XXXVIII.

Parain, Charles. "The Evolution of Agricultural Technique," CEH, I (1941), 118–68.

Patzelt, Erna. Die fränkische Kultur und der Islam mit besonderer Berück-sichtigung der nordischen Entwicklung. Eine universalhistorische Studie. Baden, 1932.

Perroy, Édouard. "Encore Mahomet et Charlemagne," *Revue historique,* CCXII (1954), 232–38.

Piganiol, André. L'Empire chrétien (325–395). Tome IV, Part II, of Histoire romaine edited by Gustave Glotz. Paris, 1947.

Pirenne, Henri. Mahomet et Charlemagne. 2d ed. Paris and Brussels, 1937.

————. "The Place of the Netherlands in the Economic History of Mediaeval Europe," EHR, II (1929), 20–40.

Popper, Karl R. The Open Society and Its Enemies. 2d ed. 2 vols. London, 1952.

Power, Eileen. Review of Bernard Miall's English translation of Pirenne, Mo-hammed and Charlemagne (New York, 1939), in EHR, X (1939–40), 60–62.

Powicke, F. M. Modern Historians and the Study of History: Essays and Papers. London, 1955.

Riising, Anne. "The Fate of Henri Pirenne's Thesis on the Consequences of the Islamic Expansion," *Classica et Medievalia,* XIII (1952), 87–130.

Rostovtzeff, Michael. "The Decay of the Ancient World and Its Economic Explanations," EHR, II (1930), 197–214.

———. Social and Economic History of the Roman Empire. Oxford, 1926.

——— (Rostowzew). Studien zur Geschichte des römischen Kolonates. Leipzig and Berlin, 1910.

Sagui, C. L. "La Meunerie de Barbegal (France) et les roues hydrauliques chez les anciens et au moyen âge," *Isis,* XXXVIII (1948), 225–31.

Salin, Édouard. La Civilisation mérovingienne d'après les sépultures, les textes et le laboratoire. Première partie: Les idées et les faits. Paris, 1949.

Salvianus. De gubernatione Dei. Edited by Franz Pauly. Vol. VIII in CSEL. Vienna, 1883.

Salvioli, Giuseppe. L'Istruzione pubblica in Italia nei secoli VIII, IX, e X. Florence, 1898.

Sánchez-Albornoz, Claudio. "España y el feudalismo carolingio. I: El prefeudalismo hispano-godo. II: Las instituciones feudales asturleonesas," SSCI, I (1954), 109–45.

Schieffer, Theodor. Winfrid-Bonifatius und die christliche Grundlegung Europas. Freiburg im Breisgau, 1954.

Segrè, Angelo. "The Byzantine Colonate," *Traditio,* V (1947), 103–33.

Settimane di studio del centro italiano di studi sull'alto medioevo. Vol. I: I problemi della civiltà carolingia (Spoleto, 1954). Vol. II: I problemi comuni dell'Europa postcarolingia (1955). Vol. III: I Goti in Occidente (1956).

Sidonius, Caius Sollius Apollinaris. Epistulae et carmina. Edited by Christianus Luetjohann. In MGH, Vol. VIII of Auctores antiquissimi. Berlin, 1887.

Simson, Otto G. von. Sacred Fortress. Byzantine Art and Statecraft in Ravenna. Chicago, 1948.

Singer, Charles. A Short History of Science. Oxford, 1941.

———; E. J. Holmyard; A. R. Hall; and Trevor I. Williams, eds. A History of Technology. Vol. II: The Mediterranean Civilizations and the Middle Ages, c. 700 B.C. to c. A.D. 1500. Oxford, 1956.

Sion, Jules. "Quelques Problèmes de transports dans l'antiquité: Le point de vue d'un géographe méditerranéen," *Annales,* VII (1935), 628–33.

Smith, Robert S. "Medieval Agrarian Society in Its Prime. Section 3. Spain," CEH, I (1941), 344–60.

Sombart, Werner. "Economic Theory and Economic History," EHR, II (1929), 1–19.

Stein, Ernst. Geschichte des spätrömischen Reiches. I: Vom römischen zum byzantinischen Staate (284–476 n. Chr.). Vienna, 1928.

——— (Ernest Stein). Histoire du Bas-Empire. Tome II: De la disparition de l'Empire d'Occident à la mort de Justinien (476–565). Paris-Brussels-Amsterdam, 1949.

Stephenson, Carl. "Feudalism and Its Antecedents in England," *American Historical Review,* XLVIII (1943), 245–65.

Stevens, Courtenay E. "Agriculture and Rural Life in the Later Roman Empire," CEH, I (1941), 89–117.

Stöckle, Albert. Spätrömische und byzantinische Zünfte. *Klio,* Beiheft IX. Leipzig, 1911.

Straub, Johannes. "Christliche Geschichtsapologetik in der Krisis des römischen Reiches," *Historia,* I (1950), 52–81.

Sullivan, Richard E. "The Carolingian Missionary and the Pagan," *Speculum,* XXVIII (1953), 705–40.

——. "Early Medieval Missionary Activity: A Comparative Study of Eastern and Western Methods," *Church History,* XXIII (1954), 17–35.

Sundwall, Johannes. Weströmische Studien. Berlin, 1915.

Thompson, E. A. A Roman Reformer and Inventor, Being a New Text of the Treatise *De rebus bellicis.* Oxford, 1952.

Thompson, James Westfall. "Profitable Fields of Investigation in Medieval History," *American Historical Review,* XVIII (1913), 490–504.

——. "Serfdom in the Medieval Campagna," in Festschrift Dopsch. Baden bei Wien, 1938.

Thorndike, Lynn. Review of A. C. Crombie, Augustine to Galileo (London, 1952), in *Speculum,* XXIX (1954), 541–45.

Thouvenot, Raymond. "Salvien et la ruine de l'Empire romain," *École française de Rome. Mélanges d'archéologie et d'histoire,* XXXVIII (1920), 145–63.

Toynbee, Arnold J. A Study of History. Vols. I–III, 2d ed., London, 1935. Vols. IV–VI, London, 1939. Vols. VII–X, London, New York, Toronto, 1954.

——. ——. Abridgment of Vols. I–VI by D. C. Somervell. New York and London, 1947.

Verlinden, Charles. L'Esclavage dans l'Europe médiévale. I: Péninsule ibérique-France. Brugge, 1955.

Vinogradoff, Paul. "Social and Economic Conditions of the Roman Empire in the Fourth Century," CMH, I (1924), 543–67.

Walbank, F. W. The Decline of the Roman Empire in the West. London, 1946.

Wallace-Hadrill, J. M. The Barbarian West 400–1000. London, 1952.

Wallach, Luitpold. "Education and Culture in the Tenth Century," *Medievalia et Humanistica,* IX (1955), 18–22.

White, Lynn T., Jr. "Technology and Invention in the Middle Ages," *Speculum,* XV (1940), 141–59.

Zulueta, Francis de. "De Patrociniis Vicorum, a Commentary on C. Th. 11, 24 and C. J. 11, 54," in *Oxford Studies in Social and Legal History,* I (1909), 1–78.

Index